S REFUGE OF ANARCHY

UNTIMELY MEDITATIONS

LAW AS REFUGE OF ANARCHY

SOCIETIES WITHOUT HEGEMONY OR STATE

HERMANN AMBORN

TRANSLATED BY ADRIAN NATHAN WEST

THE MIT PRESS
CAMBRIDGE, MASSACHUSETTS
LONDON, ENGLAND

Originally published as *Das Recht als Hort der Anarchie: Gesellschaften ohne Herrschaft und Staat* in the series *Fröhliche Wissenschaft* by Matthes and Seitz Berlin: © Matthes and Seitz Berlin Verlagsgesellschaft mbH, Berlin 2016. All rights reserved.

The translation of this work was funded by Geisteswissenschaften International— Translation Funding for Work in the Humanities and Social Sciences from Germany, a joint initiative of the Fritz Thyssen Foundation, German Federal Foreign Office, collecting society VG WORT, and Börsenverein des Deutschen Buchhandels (German Publishers and Booksellers Association).

This book was set in PF DinText Pro by Toppan Best-set Premedia Limited. Printed and bound in the United States of America.

Library of Congress Cataloging-in-Publication Data

Names: Amborn, Hermann, author.
Title: Law as refuge of anarchy : societies without hegemony or state / Hermann Amborn ; translated by Adrian Nathan West.
Other titles: Recht als Hort der Anarchie. English
Description: Cambridge, MA : MIT Press, 2019. | Series: Untimely meditations ; #15 | Includes bibliographical references.
Identifiers: LCCN 2018024748 | ISBN 9780262536585 (pbk. : alk. paper)
Subjects: LCSH: Hegemony. | Legitimacy of governments | Anarchism. | State, The.
Classification: LCC JZ1312 .A6313 2019 | DDC 327.1/14--dc23 LC record available at https://lccn.loc.gov/2018024748

10   9   8   7   6   5   4   3   2   1

CONTENTS

LAW AS REFUGE OF ANARCHY

I HEGEMONIC POWER IS NOT A UNIVERSAL

I.1. OUTLINE OF THE PROBLEM AND STATEMENT OF OBJECTIVES

"Once there was a brawl between two brothers, and one of them lost his life. The clan head found the victor responsible for the other's death, and ordered him executed. Word of this verdict reached the guilty man in his hiding place. He summoned his friends and explained to them the situation: his brother had swindled him and had beaten him afterward. During the scuffle, his brother succumbed to his wounds. The listeners then resolved to form a delegation that would address such allegations in the future. After examining the circumstances, solutions would be arrived at by common consent. From now on, they declared, the clan head could no longer decide on his own; indeed, he would henceforward be excluded from the proceedings. He would only be notified once a verdict had been reached, and his role would be merely to sanction this verdict. That happened long, long ago, and that is our tradition."

I was told this story, which allegedly took place in Ethiopia, in Gollango, to the south of Lake Chamo (long known in Europe by the name Lake Ruspoli), during a research trip to the Horn of Africa. I was speaking with my informants about our respective notions of legality and illegality, and those empowered to decide between them. Here, a few scant words suffice to portray a radical social process: the transfer of jurisdiction from a centralized authority to a multitude of responsible parties. This signified an extraordinary expansion of a basic principle of Roman law concerning fair negotiations—*audiatur et altera pars*, which no one in southern Ethiopia could have heard of—so that not only were all sides heard but the community of those present was even drawn into the judgment process. The above tale contains, in a concentrated form, all those constellations pursued in the following inquiry: power and counterpower, hegemony and resistance to hegemony, communication and conceptions of law. These processes are examined among communities where reciprocity is a dominant societal principle—communities where the interpenetration of social networks and institutions obviates the need for centralized power. They offer a counterpoint to societies with strict hierarchical structures. The people who have devised this form of life in common are acting coequals.

Communities with this form, which can be found the world over, are in no sense a historical forestage of monarchy or a primitive state. They are instead a countermodel to the state of a kind that today only persists within state borders, and therefore must confront and occasionally negotiate with state organizational structures. Sometimes these communities are small social units, but frequently they encompass millions of people. Often they have been declared dead or obsolete as a social model, yet they continue to exist, despite the dangers they face from within and without.

In the course of my inquiry, I would like to shed light on social forms of expression, emanations, ideas, practices, and institutions that oppose or at least problematize the hegemony of one group of people over another. What has particularly aroused my interest, in examining the reasons for the strength and stability of these nonhegemonic forms of communal life, is the extent to which reigning conceptions of values and laws uphold the continuity of societies with this structure, for example, by counteracting tendencies toward the accumulation of power.

My considerations depart from several brief, elementary observations concerning the many forms of human coexistence. In the course of history, people have developed manifold varieties of communal life; the state is only *one* of the possibilities for society. I will contrast state structures with nonhegemonic societies presently observable in many parts of the world, and in this connection, will give particular attention to nonhierarchical societies in the Horn of Africa.

Since British anthropologists in the 1940s first shed light on "regulated anarchist" societies in Africa, there have been continuous attempts to disparage these communities' social and political achievements. This merits mention, even if I will not enter into this particular anthropological controversy here.[1] The steadfast skepticism directed at antihegemonic movements is all the more remarkable insofar as critiques of hierarchical structures appear regularly within Western societies, which at times have been described as undergoing a fundamental crisis. Germane here are both political structures (for example, in the form of protest movements) as well as societal coexistence taken as a whole (with, say, the demand for "streamlined hierarchies" and the mediation law that came into force in 2012); here, too, stress should be laid on egalitarian tendencies evident in present-day industrial societies that highlight the relevance of this problematic.

Afterward, I will examine the nature of those communities where law has no recourse to coercion, no authority possesses a monopoly on violence, and legitimacy is granted to systems of rules elaborated by members themselves.[2] Only a detailed presentation of these societies will suffice to clarify the complex historical and sociopolitical relationships that link this peculiar form of law to nonhegemonic societies. The efficacy of the law here forms the basis for the established power relations—which are neither hegemonic nor violent; it is thus advisable to elucidate these concepts with reference to the analyses of Western theorists and philosophers concerning this theme. Their considerations will frequently prove suggestive, even when not directly apropos.

For my observations, power relationships have a twofold significance: in general, as a supportive or disruptive element within nonhegemonic societies, and in particular, in relation to the legal order. After examining the concept of law as a constituent part of the reality of life as a whole, I will look at specific legal cases and study in detail the ways that communicative action, undertaken in common, reaches consensual solutions and makes possible consent to decisions without resort to violence.

With my analysis, I would like to clarify the degree to which the nonhegemonic ethos, striving for autonomous forms, and rejection of centralized authority are reflected in law. But above all, I would like to understand how anarchic social formations can exist despite massive and manifold influences and threats. As we see in the Horn of Africa, autonomous jurisdiction, directed against destructive influences from without, contributes (even when its legitimacy is restricted to certain domains) remarkably to the stabilization of these forms of communal life, although or even because law, as established and exercised in the community, represents a counterweight to hegemonic violence.

I.2. LIFE IN COMMON: STATE VERSUS ORDERED ANARCHY

Man is a social being. Hence, man lives in society not as a consequence of virtue or in the pursuit of his interests but rather because no other form of being is possible.[3] Only within a community based on communication is personal development possible; this is something not even Robinson Crusoe can avoid. This is not to deny the possibility that tensions may arise in the ego's relationship to the community. Cooperation, assistance, and adaptation stand opposite selfishness, the striving for dominance, and expansion as the twin poles of social relations, and the cultural achievements of humanity throughout the course of history have depended on the testing out of the varieties of social relations and orders that lie between these extremes.

The Western perspective sees as victorious the hierarchization of society and societal division of labor, which have evolved from the Neolithic revolution through chiefdoms and monarchies to despotism and finally the modern state. Occidental thinkers have failed to conceive of the epoch before the state as anything other than chaos. In line with this view, in the shadow of the English Civil War, Thomas Hobbes, one of the founders of modern political philosophy, depicted in *Leviathan* a barbaric, bestial, atavistic environment where man was the wolf of man, and the war of all against all for the sake of goods and prestige was the rule. People could only break free of this condition through a contract uniting each individual will into a single common one. In addition, the honoring of contracts and execution of laws were impossible without coercion. For this reason, citizens hand over their "natural" rights to the sovereign, who reigns with unrestrained violence and subjugates all.[4] The state, embodied in the sovereign, guarantees peaceful communal life to the citizen; it is hence the precondition for a harmonious society. With *Leviathan*, Hobbes grounded in the history of ideas the monopoly on force by the state—a principle still accepted down to the present day—and his stress on the necessity of the state continues to mark the orientation system and evaluative models of political science and sociology. Thus Karl Jaspers could write, just two years after the end of the National Socialist tyranny, that communal life is "impossible without a guiding will," and requires "leadership and subordination."[5]

Two striking examples of the way contemporary political science adjudges nonstate organizational forms are Somaliland and Puntland, which have emerged in the north of Somalia; both are confined to the category of "failed state." Neither possesses a semblance of the classical nation-state with centralized competencies, a monopoly on force, and bureaucratic leadership. Political matters are instead regulated by bodies derived from the councils of elders. Even in its better days, one could at most have described colonial and postcolonial Somalia itself as an incomplete state. The achievement of those who have created functioning community structures in Somaliland and Puntland outside the state has been denied. Rather, the international community is committed to rebuilding a state in Somalia with a monopolized organizational structure like that of a Western state in the belief that this will generate greater security within and beyond its borders.

Michel Foucault analyzes the ways the state habituates the individual and imposes the social practices that constitute everyday life. This does not mean there is no alternative. The nation-state is still seen as the predominant political form across the globe, but there are indications that it has crossed its zenith. Increasingly, states seem overwhelmed by contemporary demands; they have curtailed their social responsibilities; and privatization is growing, and along with it the influence of lobbyists as well as international institutions. In his comparative studies, Trutz von Trotha demonstrates that evolution toward the state is not the historical norm, and given the multiplicity of its stipulations—a monopoly on force, bureaucratic apparatus, and so on—its propagation in other societies is a utopian ideal.[6] Attempts to institute statist hegemonies at the global level are not only utopian; they also have fatal repercussions for the praxis of those postcolonial "states"—Afghanistan is an illustration here—where military violence has tried to install neoliberal "democratic" regimes.

The emergence of the state with its claims to sovereignty is therefore only *one* among numerous options for organizing human life in common. There is no unavoidable chain of developments leading from simple family ties, where such exist, to political power as expressed in the state through relations conditioned by violence. In the end, these are simply images handed down to us from nineteenth-century evolutionism. And as ethnology shows, the nation-state with its monopoly on force is hardly the most highly differentiated extant model of sociopolitical order.

An examination of the historical conditions under which present-day nation-states arose lies outside the scope of this inquiry. I would stress, however, that the communities presented here are in no sense prestate formations requiring only another evolutionary step (to avoid redundancy) to develop from an embryonic political stage into states proper. Anthropologists are not without blame for this unilinear evolutionist perspective. For decades, their descriptions focused mainly on small groups within nonhegemonic societies and so-called hunter-gatherer bands in particular so that conceiving of larger-dimensioned forms of socializations was impossible.

Émile Durkheim and Max Weber had already explored nonstate forms of communal life on the theoretical, largely still hypothetical plane. Indeed, it was Durkheim who coined the concept of "segmentary societies" to describe those composed of homologous social elements.[7] Anthropologists took up and expanded on this concept.

More intensive research avoided societies of this type until the 1930s, when the British failed in their attempt to institute indirect rule, their customary system of colonial administration, among densely populated ethnic groups in Africa for which hierarchical organization did not exist. In indirect rule, indigenous authorities were appointed heads of administrations intended to institute and enforce orders at the behest of the colonial power. But these chiefs went unrecognized by the population at large, and no one heeded their commands. The administration found this baffling, and was unable to understand it until the anthropologists appointed by the colonial administration finally offered an explanation. Their ranks included Jack Goody, Meyer Fortes, and Edward E. Evans-Pritchard, who had researched the Nuer people of Sudan and described their social formations as "ordered anarchy."[8] The work of the British social anthropologists gave rise to heated debate. My own observations proceed from their research to explore the supportive function of law in these nonhegemonic societies. Whether societies of this type may develop hierarchies remains an open question. Harold Barclay has looked into social sectors from which a tendency to state formation might arise.[9] Many societies, for instance, reserve substantial powers for older men. Where there is gerontocracy, it is no longer possible to speak of an egalitarian society. Even a hegemony headed by elders, though, is time bound in each individual case. Peers change constantly, so that at the least, this form of institutionalized power sharing does not produce heritable dynasties.

Somewhat different is the situation of so-called Big Men—those influential figures who develop a devoted network of clients via patronage, economic support, and perhaps even heroic exploits. Where these have reached a position of despotism, many have failed to sustain it, and the community has risen up against them, at times not shying away from tyrannicide. That said, when Big Men have managed to use their political and economic position of authority as the basis for monarchy, this has often been in concert with the intrusion of imperial powers.

Even in chiefdoms, evolution does not necessarily tend toward a centralized command structure, although economic and demographic conditions may make such a thing possible. Christopher Boehm lists numerous examples of ways the power of chiefs is constrained, while Christian Sigrist affirms that "there persists, in segmentary societies, an ambivalence with regard to the prominent (such as wealthy men or authorities), which tends to reduce their functions to mere representation."[10] Last but not least, Pierre Clastres has proven conclusively with his research into the Indians of the Amazon that their form of chiefdom and its related ethical framework opposes any transition into state formation; for them, it is morally objectionable to permit one person to issue orders to others if these orders are not subject to question.[11]

Though Ralf Dahrendorf and others continued to assert in 1964 that nonhegemonic societies were impossible, these examples demonstrate that hegemony is in no way a constant among humans, however much biological—physical and mental—distinctions among individuals are invoked as bases for hierarchy and domination, and however much social inequality is postulated as "natural."[12] Ethnological examples show, as Sigrist emphasizes, that "there is no anthropological necessity for centralized sovereignty, hierarchy, exploitation, or structural inequality."[13] Alternatives are not only conceivable but also real.

The classical theorists of anarchism approached nonhegemony from a different perspective. While anthropologists describe existing nonhegemonic societies, and analyze present and future threats to them, anarchists projected the image of a stateless society to come. In doing so, they were frequently aware of descriptions of egalitarian community forms among the North American Indians—the noncentralized organization of the Iroquois councils, for instance. Thus Peter Kropotkin, in 1898, replies sarcastically to Hobbes's advocacy for state authority by affirming that if people have failings and are capable of antisocial acts, then sovereigns within that state can also not be free of failings: "To expect a reduction in antisocial acts from the erection of a state system with an organized leadership structure is to lapse into the utopian notion that leaders are faultless, good men. The entirety of historical experience teaches us otherwise."[14]

Kropotkin sees the law of mutual aid as the driving force of evolutionary progress, and his concept of society rests on the basic principle of complete equality. For him, people's natural aspiration to organize into communities can only develop in nonhegemonic societies. There, even as the freedoms and rights of others limit the freedom of the individual, the individual develops concern for others, not through compulsion, but rather on the basis of voluntary agreement.

Furthermore, as Karl Marx stresses, the other is not simply the limit of individual freedom; instead, it is only within a community of others that the individual may cultivate their aptitudes. The other is therefore a precondition of survival and existence.[15]

I.3. FREEDOM FROM HEGEMONY IN HEGEMONIC STATES

An essential contemporary reference point for me are those indigenous groups that have managed to dispense with hegemony. They exhibit great diversity across the globe, from hunter-gatherer bands where all members are acquaintances to populous ethnic groups practicing farming.[16] Still, they all share certain recognizable properties, which may be considered ideal types in Weber's sense:[17]

- Members pursue communal interests through cooperative practices, and social coexistence is subject to collective negotiating; these societies are distinguished by a high measure of personal autonomy.

- The basic principles of coexistence are mutuality and horizontal interdependence among persons endowed with equal rights. Ruptures, but also alliances (fission and fusion), frequently arise—not only through conflict—to maintain the flexibility of relations in these networks and facilitate equilibrium.

- Essential economic resources are either held in common, as property, or are subject to society's control, and wealth accumulation is not a desired outcome. Greed and envy are scorned; instead, there is an imperative to share.

Characteristic traits include reciprocity, solidarity, and the balance of power; hence vertical—hierarchical—stratification is unknown.[18] Nor is there a core organizational group with a mandate to violence or heritable political authority. When extraordinary circumstances, such as a hunt or war, bestow power on specific persons with marked leadership abilities, their authorization to lead does not extend beyond this purpose, and even there, only so long as is necessary. In general, those people called "chiefs" in Western sources are *principes inter pares*. This position is commonly entrusted to elders, granting them, among other things, a measure of authority in the settlement of disputes. Even then, they cannot force anyone to follow their orders.

Rules for coexistence clearly sustain these communities. In small societies with face-to-face relations, where individual members are controlled by those around them, mutual criticism suffices to guarantee individual members' allegiance. In large groups, where individuals can more easily evade criticism, moral precepts tend to constitute guidelines for behavior and on occasion form the basis for codified rules. During conflicts, these offer an orientation for negotiations, so that each person is not required to know everything about the others.

* * *

The distinctive cultural manifestations of individual ethnic groups and the approaches particular to each researcher mean that nonhegemonic social forms go by a variety of designations. All fall under the semantic field of anarchy, understood here literally as "nonhegemonic," and not derided under such labels as chaos, political disorder, lawlessness, and arbitrariness. Frequently, the concept "egalitarian" has described nonhegemonic societies. This notion itself has a long history. During the Enlightenment, critics of civilization and prerevolutionary thinkers like Jean-Jacques Rousseau and Baron de Lahontan sought countermodels to feudal society. They were fascinated by reports of North American Indians—the study of which led to the positing of egalitarian societal forms. With the victory of the bourgeois revolution in France, this concept lost its "projective force," and the idea of equality was relegated to the "primitive," "savage," "egalitarian" hordes, all of which were the domain of ethnology.[19]

The concept of equal rights was inherent to the novel—bourgeois—ideology of *égalité* with its stress on formal equality before the law, even as it ignored actually existing inequalities. As Marshall Sahlins—himself an admirer of stateless societies—affirms, no human society may boast of absolute equality; at the very least, roles are generally divided according to age and sex.[20] What do exist are solidaristic, reciprocal, and complementary relations.[21] As a result, in certain societies equilibrium arises among subjects and institutions in a way unknown to centralized-hierarchical ones.

"Egalitarian society" is inadequate as a taxonomic notion. There are, however, societies that strive for equivalence, nonhegemony, and equality (if only as an ideal). I will therefore resort to the adjective "egalitarian" at times, placing it in quotation marks when it describes the attributes of a given society. In these instances, the qualifier should be kept in mind. I will dispense with quotation marks for such formulations as *egalitarian tendencies* or *egalitarian ethos*.

The term "segmentary" will describe societies in which institutions stand side by side on an equal footing; these are understood as an agglomeration of segments of equivalent social rank.

Closely related to nonhegemony is the concept of anarchy, which many researchers use, especially when attempting to bring into view the structure of a society under examination, often employing the distinction of "ordered anarchy."[22]

The idea of "acephaly" applies, strictly speaking, only to groups without leadership positions. Like "tribes without rulers" or "societies without states," it expresses, in the final instance, a lack. And yet the ethnic groups concerned here do not display any lack; instead, other ontologies and epistemologies are at play. I thus refer to these as polycephalic societies, which parcel out obligations, power, authority, and competency to many "heads" across the entire society, enabling direct democracy. By dividing political and religious power domains among a multitude of people, they work against individuals' tendencies to annex power.[23]

I.4. EGALITARIAN TENDENCIES IN THE METROPOLIS

The eschewal of hierarchical political conceptions is not restricted to theory but instead is evident in the practices and attributes of protest movements in recent years. The unease many feel at the global effects of neoliberalism has led to new interest in basic democratic praxis worldwide, and at the same time has given impetus to the critique of statist representative parliamentary systems. Protests in Israel against the high costs of living, town squares occupied in Greece in opposition to austerity, Democracia Real Ya! in Spain, and even the spontaneous Occupy movement in the United States or Nuit debout in France, which rebelled against new labor laws, have attracted many followers; these and similar voluntary associations and movements distinguish themselves through self-organization, direct democracy, autonomy, and mutual aid. There is a growing multitude of decentralized organizational forms with no desire for leadership personalities. As they seek new forms of societal, political, and economic life, anarchism-inspired discussions are experiencing a renaissance.

The challenges of praxis in decentralized organizations frequently correspond to those of the nonhegemonic

societies anthropologists describe. Even plenums in protest movements struggle to reach the ideal of unanimous
decision making. It is difficult and time-consuming to reach
a consensus acceptable to all. Such was the discovery of
European colonial masters in Africa; they were exasperated
by the long and seemingly ineffective discussions there,
or else ridiculed them as "endless palaver." Their participants naturally saw things otherwise, as James Africanus
Beale Horton reported as early as 1868. Horton's father,
who had been abducted as a slave, had told him that in the
segmentary Igbo society in the Nigeria of the time, every
grown man in the village took part in assemblies and could
express his opinion without compulsion: "They would not,
as a rule, allow anyone to act the superior over them; nor
sway their conscience by coercion, to the performance of
any act, whether good or bad, when they have not the incli-
nation to do so. ... [I]n fact, everyone likes to be his own
master."[24]

While voting and majority rule may be simpler, they
encourage competitive behavior and normally leave behind
losers—with far-reaching consequences, as David Graeber
states: "Voting would be the most likely means to guarantee
humiliations, resentments, hatreds, [and] in the end, the
destruction of communities."[25] There is thus little difference
between this procedure and the implementation of decisions by force. For this reason, the vote-based democracy
promoted by Western powers has led to polarization in
many of the basic democratic societies of southern Ethiopia
and, in many cases, bloody confrontations.[26]

An awareness of nonhegemonic societies is a prerequisite for those who would advocate for the interests of indigenous population groups, and particularly for those indigenous movements that build on traditional, equality-based political forms. Further, ethnology neither can nor ought to offer recipes, but instead may promote discourse in its home countries and encourage sustained contact with outsiders. We cannot solve our own problems by simply adopting elements or structural features from existing polycephalic societies. As Sigrist already noted in 1978, these are "alternative societies for social theory—if not for immediate political praxis."[27] They do, however, confirm for him that equality and nonhegemony do not fall short of the demands of anthropology. In the interim, many approximations between theory and praxis have taken place, with the autonomous communes in Chiapas marking the first cycle of the new global upheaval, according to Graeber. The Zapatistas did not permit themselves to be reduced to Indians demanding autonomy. They repudiated "the idea of seizing power and [attempted] instead to create a model of democratic self-organization to inspire the rest of Mexico [initiating] an international network."[28] They succeeded in bringing together indigenous people, activists, *and* scholars to carry out discussions with global validity.[29]

If we look to our own society for further manifestations of egalitarianism, the internet, with its "anarchic" structure, comes immediately to mind. More surprising, though, are borrowings patterned on indigenous models in domains that can hardly be described as revolutionary or anarchic. An example is Germany's Mediation Act, which entered into vigor in July 2012, and resembles social entities in which the fundamental tendency is toward conflict resolution through common accord rather than resort to a codex of fixed regulations that generate authorized rulings to which affected parties are compelled to submit. This German law, redacted in accordance with European Parliament guidelines, is a rightful, valid alternative form of conflict resolution. Its goal is "on a voluntary basis and autonomously, to achieve an amicable resolution of their conflict" (§ 1). The drafters of this law could have transcribed this word for word from mediation proceedings in southern Ethiopia.[30]

For some time now, doubts have emerged as to the general validity and effectiveness of hierarchical structures in the economy. Economists themselves have been the source of fundamental impulses for organizational innovations based on anarchist ideas once derided as utopian. Greater cooperation in work groups is now a desideratum, as are simultaneous engagement in politics, economy, and research. Now we hear talk of slimmed-down hierarchies or lean management, along with demands for more vertical permeability. "Complex interaction" among different groups inside and outside organizations is now seen as worth striving for; the dismantling of hegemony has become a means of profit maximization, with the emancipation of fellow workers as a secondary effect.[31]

I.5. EGALITARIAN RELATIONS WORLDWIDE
I.5.1. Global Distribution

The prevailing opinion since the nineteenth century, which has held nonhegemonic social formations to be "primitive" and doomed to decline, has no historical or contemporary basis in fact. Of course, many nonhegemonic societies have disappeared; all have suffered under colonial and global transformations, and have faced political pressure the world over. Yet some politicians, like President Julius Nyerere in Tanzania decades ago, have come to see that such social forms are neither archaic nor inimical to modern development—in Uganda, for example, or Ethiopia, which has formalized this recognition in its federal constitution.

Nonetheless, insight and realpolitik often diverge widely. Almost everywhere, the problems faced by societies with nonstatist administrations have led to radical changes. But despite or perhaps because of attempts to institute hierarchical structures, the fundamental principles and worldviews underlying social interaction in common continue to be in force. In some places, they have risen to prominence, and in others, they are forced into the background. Between the poles of "equality" and repressive hegemony lies a multitude of variants and crossovers; reality shirks strict classifications.

The vitality and pragmatism that contemporary anarchy is capable of are evident in northern Somalia and among the Zapatistas in Chiapas, but also among the Tallensi of northern Ghana as well as numerous ethnic groups in the south and east of Africa.[32] Also instructive are social movements in Argentina at the dawn of the twenty-first century. After neoliberal economic policies drove the country into a profound crisis, mass protests arose, and from them, neighborhood councils emerged with basic democratic organizational forms that have at times played a decisive role in the political life of Argentina. These movements strove for social equality, autonomy, and solidarity, and rejected conventional representative democracy. They succeeded thanks to the networks they established and their high rate of participation, dealing with problems in the community and restarting factories abandoned by their owners. These networks' status was at least as significant a force in Argentine politics as the system of representative, pluralistic democracy.[33] Reviled by the conservative media, the movement began to flag in 2004; not only had the regime in power fomented internal strife, but the economic rebound had led to improvements in the situation of the middle class. According to Raina Zimmering, however, "a fund of expertise and perspectives has accumulated among the various layers of society, the effects of which will long be felt, and which can be reactivated at any time."[34]

Ute Luig confirms Sigrist's thesis that consciousness of equality has remained determinant over long spans of time and that power balances are inscribed within acephalic structures.[35] With the example of the Tonga in Zambia, she confirms that inequality may only persist temporarily in segmentary societies. Up to now, colonial and postcolonial political structures have barely altered the inner balance of power and counterpower. "The structures of acephaly and the accompanying awareness of equality continue to dominate the political structures of public consciousness, at least at the local level."[36]

Charles Macdonald goes further than Sigrist or Luig in positing the stability of equality as a facet of human consciousness. For him, the peaceable Palawan communities of the southern Philippines are paradigmatic for anarchic societies in which autonomous individuals arrange collective life flexibly. Macdonald divides "egalitarian" societies into systems of anarchic group formation (anarcho-gregarious regimes) and open gatherings of individuals responding to contingent demands (randomly arranged open aggregates). To him, both forms are older than societies with fixed structures and ordering systems, and are anchored in the depths of human consciousness. Historically and ethnographically corroborated "anarcho-social regimes" are not a forestage but rather the core of numerous collective undertakings even within modern statist societies.[37] Illustrations include concepts of social complexity, contingent arrangements, and spontaneous associations like those that arise in the wake of catastrophes. All this expresses a basic human need for commonality that opposes any sort of imbalance.

Pierre Clastres's investigations into the indigenous populations of the Amazon Basin are among the most significant field studies of stateless societies of the neocolonial era. These are not mere case studies. Their importance reaches further, given that for many years, research into egalitarian societies has owed its essential impulse to his ethnological-philosophical reflections. As questions of power stand at the center of Clastres's considerations, I will only touch on them in detail in section II.4.

A "regression" from hierarchical to acephalic relations is also possible, as when the assemblies of tribal chiefs instituted in the colonial period vanished with the coming of independence.[38] Graeber offers a striking instance of the transition from monarchy to egalitarian structures: in the nineteenth century, no one in Madagascar questioned the legitimacy of the monarchy, but the French authorities considered the monarchs immoral, as they had enslaved a part of the population. This view appears to have been applied to state organizations in general, leading to passive resistance against state institutions along with the formation of autonomous and relatively egalitarian forms of self-administration.[39]

In southern Ethiopia during the 1974 revolution, the "socialist" Derg administration dissolved the post of *balabat* (administrative chief) that the imperial powers had instated and introduced another rigid institution with the right of recourse to state authority. Interestingly, when the Derg were overthrown, the *balabat* were unable to return to power; local populations instead returned to polycephalic principles, which the current regime has retained. Processes of this kind refute the idea of unilinear evolution; in lieu of an evolution from anarchy to centralized authority, we have multiple evolutionary strands running in different directions. The question of nonhegemonic institutions has also engaged African intellectuals. Philosophers like Kwasi

Wiredu, Bénézet Bujo, and Egosa Osaghae offer critical examinations of traditional basic democratic models with egalitarian decision-making processes as well as proposals for ways that this heritage may be fruitfully integrated into modern ones.[40]

Among those groups intent on equality are a majority of the indigenous peoples belonging to the UN Permanent Forum on Indigenous Issues. These work to preserve their rights in industrial states and emerging economies. The First Nations of Canada are an example of this, including their website Mostly Water.[41] The articles that appear on that site, composed by indigenous authors, do not refer exclusively to Canada. This shows that the struggle for statelessness and horizontal, immanent life-forms is a current one.[42] Anarchy is not a project or utopia but rather a thing being put into practice.[43]

In Africa, the situation is different. While polycephalic societies are fundamentally distinct from state structures at the local level, their ties to the state are frequently stronger together than in industrial nations. A West African friend expressed this to me perceptively: "The citizen and the native cross paths through my body."

I.5.2. Nonhegemonic Societies in the Horn of Africa

The capacity of equality-oriented societies to endure in the face of *progressive* political, social, economic, and societal structures is evident among many people residing in the Horn of Africa to the south of Addis Ababa. In contrast to the dominant Amhara and Tigre in Ethiopia, who view themselves as upholders of the state, the former cling to nonhegemonic structures.

Certain characteristics of these societies are of fundamental importance for the theoretical considerations in part II and therefore will be presented here briefly as a prelude to their in-depth examination in part III.

The ethnic groups explored here were subjugated around 1900 by Emperor Menilek's troops and have long been incorporated into the Ethiopian state. They reacted to the influence of state power with an interesting array of responses. The Oromo in the Gibe region to the north of Kaffa developed several forms of monarchy, while the better part of the other southern Ethiopian Oromo groups and eastern Cushitic speakers rejected a centralized ordering of society and maintained their polycephalic structures, which they deemed well suited to them.[44] In any case, the designation of a society as polycephalic or hierarchical-centralized should not be viewed as essential but rather as one possibility along a continuum. There existed points of contact with the hierarchically structured, formerly religious monarchies of the Omotic-speaking peoples, among whom the Kaffa, lying in the northern Ethiopian sphere of influence, were the most powerful and expansive. Indeed, a multitude of sociopolitical variants is characteristic of ethnic groups in the Horn of Africa.

And yet there too the egalitarian basic principles of nonhegemonic societies described above are valid. The societies of the Horn of Africa are highly populous, so face-to-face relations play a lesser role. They are segmented into small communities that see themselves in a larger context. The Burji, for example, organize a yearly international All Burji Assembly, and the Borana, who inhabit an area of Ethiopia and Kenya approximately the same size as Greece, come together every eight years in a meeting with some three thousand participants to discuss legal and social problems.

For the ethnic groups I have presented, *polycephalic societies* is the most adequate designation. In their ideal form, these consist of interlocked, reciprocal, and coequal sectors. Their reciprocity comes through clearest in their dual relations (see next paragraph), and coequality exists for individual members both socially and politically. On the basis of these characteristics and their conscious dissociation from authoritarian regimes, these societies' particularities must be viewed in a broader framework: the semantic field of anarchy.

The important institutions in these societies are the territorial unit, lineage or clan, and generation grading system. The territorial unit encompasses all people, irrespective of age or sex. Following the principle of duality, such settlement societies are frequently divided into halves that stand in a simultaneously antagonistic and interdependent relation to one another. Lineages and clans comprise unilinear descent groups whose members understand one another as kin. They are exogamously organized; that is, their members are not free to intermarry. As a general rule in segmentary societies, these individual subsystems with their territorial and relational modes of organization are considered coequal.

In addition, people are grouped by generation into a system known as the "Gada." In this framework, they pass at fixed intervals through an established succession of rankings that determine the individual's status and function. It is not a person's biological age, as in the age-set system, that determines social maturity but rather their genealogical position. The system is complex, underwent radical changes in the previous century, and continues to exist in some regions only in a rudimentary form. Its egalitarian values have survived, however, along with a derived ethos that persists in the discussion style of Gada groups and the ways their members conduct themselves together. Among Oromo intellectuals, basic democratic ideals associated with the Gada system have recently gained in significance. In contrast to the centrally organized peoples of northern Ethiopia, for them, the Gada system has become a rallying cry and symbol of their identity.

An adult man belongs to all three systems and can exercise authority in all three. But these different social domains or institutions may pursue divergent interests, so that subjects often encounter decision-making dilemmas. The thematizing and working through of tensions and conflicts that arise in the social fabric from the contradictions immanent in the system is thoroughly desirable. Negotiating conflict as a group encourages social cohesion and presents the opportunity to creatively modify obsolescent structures.[45] The dialectical tension between fixed, heritable clan or lineage and the temporally variable Gada and territory system with its elected representatives keeps the whole in movement while impeding any single sector from achieving dominance. In polycephalic societies, politics is ubiquitous, and all members, but particularly men, are expected to engage one another socially and politically, to reach decisions in the domains described above as well as play a role in framing political and judicial problems. In these societies, a person acts as *homo politicus*, and this was essential to their ability to sustain their nonhegemonic form for centuries alongside monarchies—from which they consciously cordoned themselves off—and resist, for more than 120 years, enormous political and economic pressures from the extremely hierarchical and centralized dominant society to the north.

Occupiers from the north of Ethiopia stripped away these ethnic groups' independence, but locally, they succeeded in preserving a large degree of judicial autonomy despite the existence of a superordinate legal system, and this has had positive effects for their interior political relations. *Local* here should not be taken to mean small in scale; the local networks of the Borana extend across regions measuring over a thousand square kilometers.

The integration of each adult into the sociopolitical and judicial systems enables these societies to react vigorously to external influences. And yet this desired personal engagement holds forth dangers in nonhegemonic societies because individuals are urged to distinguish themselves. Through the course of their lives, adults are expected to assimilate socially relevant knowledge and strive for a wisdom that will allow them to exercise authority—and while they should employ these capacities positively, for the common good, in councils and tribunals, they can also use them for personal advantage.

There are additional informal alliances; most significant among them is the *fuld'o*, the basic democratic association of craftspeople that first arose as a reaction to oppression by the north Ethiopian occupiers, and whose male and female members possess equal rights.[46] Other informal alliances include networks based mostly on personal initiative. It is essential that relationships be horizontal, among equals. Enduring social bonds are constituted through socially and economically relevant ties of reciprocity (bond friendship) within which friends are obliged to aid one another.

We can imagine these various networks, which often transcend the borders of ethnicity, as a gigantic rhizome. It offers actors a large stage on which to react to all sorts of influences with flexibility and dynamism. Occasionally the rhizome even presents possibilities of withdrawing from state power.

Dignitaries, who are conceded special rights and powers, either by inheritance or common agreement, pose a particular danger in these equality-based societies. The law places limits on their attempts to broaden these rights and powers, but a concentration of influence is hypothetically possible. This occurs only rarely, and the question of why is central to the present study. At this point, I may propose two hypotheses. First, the broad diffusion and diversification of power functions and temporal restrictions on such functions counteract the danger of the repressive accumulation of power on the part of individuals. Second, through their everyday comportment, individuals in these societies thwart the emergence of repressive, socially viable power, even as influence and prestige remain worthy objects of aspiration. Their socialization accustoms them to encountering opposing opinions and showing respect for the dignity and autonomy of others in spite of their differences. Respect for others' autonomy and striving for an equilibrium of interests are fundamental ethical principles here. They provide the context for configurations of the ownership of material goods; excessive wealth is perceived as unseemly because it may lead equals to engage in conduct that gives rise to inequality.

There is no doubt that these institutions and the behaviors they encourage are effective instruments against hegemonic paternalism. The question remains, however, whether legal safeguards and supports are not also necessary.

I.5.3. In Flux: The Ethnology of Law, Legal Pluralism, and Indigenous Law

From the beginnings of anthropology to the present, local, traditional law, anchored partly in ethnic identity, as well as its points of comparison with the occidental legal order have been the major themes of the anthropology of law, which crystallized quite early into its own specialized domain. Its developmental threads are linked above all with the names Johann Jakob Bachofen, Henry Maine, Bronisław

Malinowski, Richard Thurnwald, Max Gluckman, and Paul Bohannan.

Functionalists like Malinowski and Thurnwald in the 1920s and 1930s researched interactions between law and society. Thurnwald recognized the significance of reciprocity as a basis for the human sense of justice and law in general.[47]

A later, more nuanced approach would act as a corrective to that formulation, which at times appeared essentialist, in structural functionalist terms. In particular, a distinction was made between the nature of the law and the expectations that it embodied; research homed in on the realities of law, with attention given to the question of who merited decision-making powers.[48] For a long time, conflict resolution stood at the center of this research, and then, from the 1970s onward, sex relations, religion, environmentalism, and human rights came to greater prominence. State influence in various legal fields as well as their reciprocal interconnections became significant themes. In 1978, Sally Moore shed light on historical development processes along with bases for changes to or annulments of the law.

Despite globalization and the consequent exportation of Western legal forms and transnational influences, all of which tend toward legal homogenization, a contrary development is observable at the local level, with an impulse toward the differentiation of legal forms tending to legal pluralism. Traditional laws and institutions are not vanishing but instead are revived. Two explanatory approaches apply here. One affirms that in those areas where the modern state has either forfeited or only weakly implemented its hegemonic power, legal uncertainty has led to the revitalization of local courts. Overlooked local forms of legitimation have long functioned alongside the state, but given its dominance, they have received little attention from researchers. The second approach sees the resurrection of traditional laws primarily as a reaction to the paternalism inherent in economic, cultural, and legal globalization, and a search for an autonomous identity. Both approaches consider traditional law a relic of the past. De facto, then, this is about "contemporary processes oriented toward the future … which to a great degree are related to problems and praxis and aim to reorder social, economic, and political relations," and as such, stand partly in concert with and partly in opposition to state authorities.[49]

Even in the Federal Republic of Germany, complementary judicial praxis has come about in the form of Islamic parallel courts in Berlin, though the German justice system views them with suspicion. This is not yet legal pluralism, and only pretrial mediation has attained a degree of legitimacy.[50]

* * *

The status of differentiated legal forms in southern Ethiopia is as follows: after the conquest by imperial Abyssinia at the end of the nineteenth century, both imperial and indigenous law existed in the occupied south, in what is now southern Ethiopia. To speak of legal pluralism would be euphemistic;

the two systems were mutually antagonistic and rejected any points of contact. For indigenous peoples, state law was a threat, and until the ouster of Haile Selassie in 1974, the *shanqella* (a derogatory term roughly equivalent to "dirty nigger" employed by representatives of the regime) were left to settle their quarrels among themselves. Members of polycephalic societies who accused another before an imperial court stepped outside their own societies. Under the Derg in the 1970s and 1980s, local cadres were wary of derision, but even in the smallest communities they imposed legal conditions that they designated as "socialist."[51]

One can only speak of pluralism proper after the adoption of the new Ethiopian Constitution, which authorizes official local judicial systems.[52] Confrontations do arise, but there is also a fruitful reciprocity, as is clear from the Fuld'o, whose resolutions were recognized as binding by the state court in Konso. In the area of Ada'a-Liben to the south of Addis Ababa, legal pluralism draws on Oromo and Amharic local law.[53] Both legal forms are applied simultaneously in stratified proceedings that place greater emphasis on Oromo law. Trials for criminal infractions remain the domain of state courts throughout the federal territory. But local courts operate in parallel for the purpose of determining compensation. The same is true in northern Kenya. Presently, as Wolbert Smidt confirms, the significance of traditional law in Ethiopia for the stability and self-organization of local communities is underestimated and seen as antagonistic to modern administration; still, state institutions do resort to it in order to resolve minor legal matters.[54]

Newer studies dismantle the dualism between legal models and praxis that predominates in many writings in the field. These "process-oriented approaches" have led to new perspectives on law according to which what we describe as a legal model must be understood as a resource mobilized by actors in a give and take of interests only concretized through practical engagement. It is a resource employed, in other words, to legitimate the interests of actors or groups and buttress them from a moral perspective. With this view, researchers turn their focus to the pursuit of individual, self-serving interests, such as indemnity or compensation in postcolonial societies. At issue here are strategies; legal conceptions are of secondary importance.[55] But are those who put forth these ideas not imposing their own ethnocentrism again through the notion of the self-serving individual pursuing the maximization of profit?

My own frame of reference is different: I examine law not as a means of implementing self-interest but rather as a conception of community and life in common that reflects an egalitarian ethos. Its subjects must interact dynamically with a variable political environment based on hegemony. I reflect, in the final analysis, on the classics of the anthropology of law, whose goal was to comprehend the relations between law and society. Beyond that, I look at the propensity to anarchy present in many of these relational systems, following discursive lines taken up repeatedly in the course of time, which remain relevant in the present day.

II POWER AND VIOLENCE, POWER AND LAW

II.1. MONOPOLIES OF VIOLENCE

In his essay "The Critique of Violence," Walter Benjamin offers a perceptive analysis of the relations between violence and law.[1] The legal, the destructive, violence, and law constitute one another mutually, in Benjamin's view, whether through authoritarian regimes, legal contracts, or even parliamentary democracies, which regulate their affairs with the mere appearance of an absence of violence. For Benjamin, law-making generates power and to that extent, is a direct manifestation of violence. Moreover, he holds the distinction between natural and positive law to be irrelevant; for him, when it comes to the implementation of violence, they are in essence the same thing. The violent enactment of law culminates in the state police apparatus, the codification of law is hierarchical at its core, and the submission of the citizen to the law is a lawful end (*Rechtszweck*). Though Benjamin sees the law as rooted fundamentally in violence, he also glimpses in it the advent of a humane sphere in which trust may arise through communication and understanding, and conflicts may be resolved without violence.

Law as a means of subordination is most drastically evident in the legal circumstances of the Third Reich. In the mid-1930s, an explosion of laws took place, among them numerous civil and administrative decrees that remain in force today, although many other laws issued at the time now inspire loathing. Law enabled senior leadership to enforce its ideology with violence and to legitimate and consolidate its positions. One need only recall the Law for the Protection of German Blood and Honor, passed in September 1935, or the Law for the Protection of Hereditary Health of October 1935, not to mention related ordinances legalizing mass murder. As Benjamin had written a decade before, a "ghastly mixture" of law and edicts arose within the police apparatus, when the SS was attached to it during the Third Reich.[2] This did not prevent Carl Schmitt from stressing the legal basis of the state. After 1942, when Adolf Hitler declared himself the supreme judge of the German people, it was no longer possible to speak of an independent judiciary. Schmitt had foreseen this development in an essay of 1934: "The true leader (*Führer*) is also always a judge. Judgeship flows from leadership."[3] Here a circle closes, as according to Georges Sorel, in the beginning, all law was the prerogative of kings and the powerful.[4]

All that is in the past, but has the law lost its violent character in the interim? Jean and John Comaroff describe a virtual fetishization of law in postcolonial states, which deploy it as an instrument of oppression in favor of political elites. In them, politics increasingly impends on the judicial realm, and ever-stronger laws sustain the free market while reinforcing the stark separation between the affluent and poor. For the authors, Benjamin's analysis proves true: "Lawmaking is power making."[5]

Acceptance of the state monopoly on force and, concomitantly, legislation is taken for granted in the modern world. One need only think of Max Weber's depiction of the state as a sovereign relation of some over others borne up by legitimate violence. Yet the relation between the polity and law has been the subject of frequent reflection since the ancients, such as in the conception of human rights as a protection for individuals in the Western sense against the arbitrariness of the state.

Is the state's monopoly on force ubiquitous? Is it only possible to maintain social order with the aid of organs of control furnished with recourse to power? How, without such organs of control, is the implementation of acknowledged laws and order possible? Occidental theorists of anarchism who aspire to nonhegemonic societies have offered passionate and controversial arguments as to how and by what means order might be established.[6]

Among my core questions is how law becomes legitimate in real polycephalic societies where the monopoly on violence does not exist. This requires a clarification of what people in these societies perceive as legitimate and what solutions they arrive at for problems when rifts occur. I would like to put forth the thesis that law has an ambivalent character: depending on the social environment, it may promote the adoption and stabilization of hegemonic relations, or—and this is essential—place restrictions on the accumulation of power. The questions then arise whether authority is always comparable to hegemony, and whether there are positive aspects to power in relation to a given society.

Pierre Clastres, the French ethnologist and theorist of modern anarchic societies, establishes categorically that no societies exist without power relations, and "coercive" power is only one particular type of power.[7] Polycephalic societies do not lack power relations; hence it is vitally to grasp how they understand and apportion access to power. Obviously caution is advised when examining claims to validity and applicability for the results of analyses carried out by theoreticians from our own societies with regard to non-Western ones. Still, the philosophical insights that they provide may offer a basis from which to approach "foreign" phenomena, especially as the frontiers between occidental and foreign conceptions are increasingly porous.[8] The following sections will make it clear how far contributions from Western theorists, particularly Michel Foucault and Hannah Arendt, may prove fruitful in the systematic investigation of power relations and power relations systems in polycephalic societies.

II.2. FOUCAULT: SUBJECT, POWER RELATIONS, AND THE INTERNALIZATION OF NORMS

Foucault views considerations of power as bound up invariably with the question of how the person has been constituted as a subject throughout history in the occidental world. According to him, this constituent process involves historical events and power relations with divergent modes of operation that leave their mark on individuals. In this way, he reinterprets the concept of the autonomous self-production of the occidental subject that has predominated from the time of the Enlightenment.

Foucault's analysis does not put forth a systematic, monolithic model of power but instead approaches the theme through numerous developmental steps and from several different vantage points. His first attempts to define power show up in early in his inquiries into the traits of discourse analysis. Later, his interest will shift to power relations and structures—that is, to a notion of power that is conceivable only in relational terms. With time, he will understand power as a principle of history, and in his last statements prior to his death, it is an ongoing, creative aspect of human action in relation to others, which may and indeed must be depicted within concrete historical constellations.[9]

In his most productive phase, Foucault drew on Friedrich Wilhelm Nietzsche to elaborate a genealogical method that would retrace historical evolutionary strands. There, power is no longer the repressive domain of discourse, but rather is rooted in the production of discourses by the self-immanent motive force of the will to power.

This leads Foucault to develop a triadic concept of power in which the historic and transitory are interrelated, and this manifests itself initially in the law:

- The first form, common in absolutism, arises in nondiscursive, repressive practices of exclusion, such as internment and public execution. The monarch demonstrates his unobstructed hegemony on the body of the delinquent.
- The second form safeguards "democratic" society with its humanistic, enlightened language of justice. Here,

offenses are understood as infractions against universal human reason and no longer as an offense to the world order that the sovereign embodies. Moreover, the person who oversteps norms may be endowed with reason and thus accorded the capacity for self-improvement through understanding. While exclusion through incarceration continues to exist, punishment is now meant to deter and rehabilitate. Insight and disciplinary measures aim to inspire conformity.

- In the third form, the common one at present, discursive and nondiscursive disciplinary methodologies and practices are united. According to Foucault, these power structures ensure a productive augmentation of forces of the kind found in factory work and the military.[10]

The second of these is of principal importance for my theme, as analogies will show. In it, disciplinary power, which forms the self-responsible subject and influences all domains of society, is key. Strikingly, Foucault sees this as manifest in carceral structures where wardens in a central watchtower can gaze into every cell unnoticed. Power is epitomized in the individual prisoner's ever-present uncertainty as to whether he is under observation, which eventually compels him to act as if this were constantly so.

Foucault transfers this behavior to social situations in general, in which subjects feel themselves accountable to control, whether by teachers, judges, supervisors, or police. The end consequence is that individuals submit to constant self-inspection. This internalized societal discipline, according to Foucault, sets in motion the process of self-reflective becoming that is the subjectivization of modern man. Through voluntary adoption of a set of practices, individuals learn to see themselves as autonomous rational beings *precisely because* they have unconsciously integrated and internalized—or as Pierre Bourdieu would say, habituated—societal practices of surveillance and acculturation as a part of their own self.[11]

How, though, does power express itself? If institutions like schools and prisons are examples of disciplinary power, then power is insubstantial and not a force that people may resort to. It is an energetic property of human practice and thought bound to reciprocal relations. It acts on others, but is not just the manipulation of the other; instead, it is closely related to others' freedom. Through these relations of power, humans incorporate themselves into society.

Foucault describes power as omnipresent, but not as a closed system. It is not a repressive or proscriptive authority that asserts itself from above onto those below by means of judicially sanctioned violence, nor is it the exercise of a prerogative to violence. In contrast to hegemonic societies with their ossified hierarchical forms, he posits power "from below" and "from within," which develop out of the power relations occurring in families, groups, and institutions.[12] And yet if power is distinct from hegemony, it is often found in its vicinity. Even when compulsion is forgone, the powerful must continually convince themselves of their own power and demonstrate it to the powerless.[13]

In the 1980s, in his late phase, Foucault again revised his concept of power and assigned the individual a broader sphere of action in society. In this view, the subject is no longer constituted through more or less consciously effectuated discourses and power relations, but instead through behavior (relation of the self to the self) with regard to power, knowledge, and ethics.

The concept of power will henceforth designate "relations between partners (... an ensemble of practices that mutually invoke and respond to one another)," and "to live in society means in any case to live in such a way that people may have an impact on their practices."[14] Correspondingly, power relations consist of "a kind of practice which does not directly or immediately act upon others, but rather upon their practices. Practices upon practices, upon possible or real, eventual or contemporary practices."[15] With the structuring of *possibilities of practice*, power stands opposed to sovereignty and violence: "A relation of violence ... forces, bends, breaks, destroys: it excludes all possibilities, and no other opposite pole remains for it save passivity." If a relationship of violence meets with resistance, it must overcome it.[16] In relationships of power, however, the other remains, attempts at influence do not abrogate recognition of the other as the subject of practice, and this opens up an entire field of responses, reactions, and agency.[17] Power thus has productive effects to the degree that discourse inevitably—possibly even subversively—engenders counterdiscourse. Given this, under certain historical circumstances, anarchic resistance to the institutional consolidation of power relations may occur.

Understood in this way, power allows for myriad possibilities for action and generates a free space wherein individual capacity to choose arises. It may therefore have its basis in individual consent or be subject to refusal. This freedom to consent at once conditions power and potentially dismantles it, if need be. But if power relations ossify in a certain direction, they are transformed into relations of hegemony.

* * *

In order to make profitable use of Foucault in the inquiry into non-Western societies, the following must be kept in mind: Foucault's genealogy of the construction of the European subject is based on an occidental concept of the individual that has predominated from the time of the Enlightenment. Ethnological research, then, must begin with the analysis of conceptions of the person in the societies in question. In polycephalic societies, individuals are not in any sense absorbed into a mandated collective that robs them of their particular qualities; rather, the culture continues to present them with a broad range of practices. This is worth noting in the deployment of nonhegemonic discourses, in which power relations permit the liberation of positive drives that generate social realities, as will be seen below.

II.3. ARENDT: ACTION IN COMMON, POWER VERSUS VIOLENCE

Arendt, like Foucault, emphasizes the creative facets of power and opposes these explicitly to violence. In doing so, she blames thinkers on the Left and Right for equating power and violence, or taking violence to be the most blatant manifestation of power. For Weber, for example, power means "the chance to impose one's own will even *against* opposition within a social relation."[18] Comparable statements can be found in the writings of Bertrand de Jouvenel, Voltaire, and Jean-Paul Sartre.

Unlike Foucault, Arendt foregrounds societal and individual—and even communicative—action, along with their effects on societal relations and politics. Her aim is to not only critically analyze existing relations but also outline possibilities for other configurations of communal life. Certain of her pronouncements in this regard, especially her considerations on the ideal form of participatory democracy, show astonishing parallels to sociopolitical operations in polycephalic societies.[19] Arendt draws on the Greek polis at the time of Aristotle and the Roman civitas to elaborate her conceptual framework, and in this way presents clear distinctions between the concepts of power, strength, force, authority, and violence.[20]

Power "corresponds to the human ability not just to act but to act in concert. Power is never the property of an individual; it belongs to a group and remains in existence only so long as the group keeps together."[21] When an individual person possesses power, he is empowered by a group.

Strength, in contrast, always redounds to and is a property of the individual. The use of the concept *force* is restricted to *natural forces* or metaphoric formulations. *Authority* consists of competencies that can be vested in a person or an office. "Its hallmark is unquestioning recognition by those who are asked to obey."[22] It demands neither compulsion nor suasion, but respect. Its antagonist is not enmity but rather contempt or mockery. I would like to add that polycephalic societies concede a *credit* to those endowed with authority, who must demonstrate themselves worthy. A person may acquire authority through insight or a capacity for sharp judgments, but not through conferral.[23] In the end, *violence* is "distinguished by its instrumental character."[24] Its implementation requires instruments (if only truncheons). Violence stands alongside strength, which serves it by multiplying the efficiency of organic instruments.

Power, as Arendt stresses, belongs to the essence and origin of all communal life—indeed, of all organized groups; it is inherent to them, and founds and maintains them. It arises whenever people act in common and requires no explicit warrant.[25] While violence always has to serve an end, which justifies and channels its employment, what power requires is legitimation. This comes not from the ends and purposes that the group advances; instead, it stems from power's origins, which are coeval with the group's formation, and derive their validity from an appeal to the past and a will to cohesion. More than a mere invocation of foundation myths detached from the present, it demands constant communication and communal practice.

Praxis, in turn, can only take place in the presence of another subject. Its preconditions are the plurality of human life and respect for that plurality. Praxis here is understood strictly as politically relevant action in the service of the polity. Praxis in this sense includes linguistic acts that steer and coordinate "normal" practices into ordered trajectories— promises to act in common in the future, as codified in covenants, contracts, and the like. Seen in this way, speech and praxis are political activities that preserve a community in the course of its everyday political existence.

Already in the Greek polis, to be political meant "everything was decided through words and persuasion and not through force and violence."[26]

Linguistic practices constitute "communicative power." This is not a mere by-product of practical reason, of reason directed toward appropriate comportment in a given environment, but is above all an outgrowth of "aesthetic" judgments that constitute a reflection on the particular: because people take different perspectives on the same things in the world that they have built in common, a form of judgment is necessary that does justice to all pluralities and yet makes the decision that eventually prevails acceptable to all.[27] For Arendt, Immanuel Kant's aesthetic judgment is an example of this.

Judgment is a subjective act only possible in the community because the human spirit "will not function outside human society."[28] It is hence "reflective judgment," unrestricted by mediation through concepts or systems. Aesthetic judgment addresses special instances for which there may well be no rule at hand.

It is based on experience that may be filtered through the experiencer's context and history, but cannot simply follow from a general rule.

The particular judgment in this instance is not an implementation of judgment in its general form but rather anterior to it. It is for this reason that Arendt distinguishes "reflective judgment" from judgments that "subsume," that depart from a premise that generates conclusions about a given case. Reflective judgment takes effect when determinant judgment is overwhelmed, and a suitable concept or concrete object is unavailable. In the absence of an applicable rule, reflective judgment must develop from the case at hand, yet it cannot be reduced a judgment of taste because it must prove acceptable for others.[29] This demands a position of "*outside-ness*, from which we pass judgment on objects and events, and do so from beyond the economy of convention and of the causal nexus."[30]

For Arendt, thinking presupposes the capacity to relinquish one's own will and adopt the standpoint of the other, which is not one's *own*—that is, to incorporate distinct points of view with regard to the same object into one's *own* thinking. Resultant judgments will rely, as Kant has stressed, neither on a specific internalized moral conception nor on empathy or identification with the opinion of the majority, but rather will be the outcome of a process.

> I form an opinion by considering a given issue from different viewpoints, by making present to my mind the standpoints of those who are absent; that is, I represent them. ... [T]his is a question neither of empathy, as though I tried to be or to feel like somebody else, nor of counting noses and joining a majority but of being and thinking in my own identity where actually I am not. The

more people's standpoints I have present in my mind while I am pondering a given issue, and the better I can imagine how I would feel and think if I were in their place, the stronger will be my capacity for representative thinking and the more valid my final conclusions, my opinion.[31]

Judgments thus ascertained have "subjectively general validity," yet do not generate principles for action.[32] They rather open a space from which to observe objects and problems in new, unfamiliar ways. This opening is not a logical activity but instead an imaginative and ideally creative one. It not only changes and augments our sense of the reality around us; it shows possible modalities and objects of communication.[33]

Accepting such judgments upholds the experience of shared sensibility as pleasure: "We find joy in that which we assert and represent."[34] In negotiations involving speakers in many African societies, there is an assigned listener who will repeat contentedly, by way of confirmation, the last half sentence of the speaker, unless consensus flags, and then he is free to express disapproval. Among the Burji of southern Ethiopia, acceptable judgments must be "beautiful, honest, and correct" (k'ajeel)—in other words, aesthetic in the final analysis.[35]

Although both Kant and Arendt proceed from the universal validity of "human judgment" as they analyze it, any analogy to judgment procedures customary in polycephalic societies must remain hypothetical. Undoubtedly, rational discussion with an appeal to prior cases stands in the foreground of decision making: What will be looked on as right and proper, and what not? Yet situations constantly arise in which precedents offer no guidance. Though "tradition" is subject to continual reflection and transformation, it frequently offers scant orientation vis-à-vis the radical changes that these societies have faced over the last hundred years. Unprecedented, novel situations demand a reflective judgment with no basis beyond individuals' own discernment.

Once arrived at, how are judgments enforced? According to Arendt, obedience depends on the agreement of the many, and positive laws, as an outgrowth of communicative power, are the precondition for ordered (republican) life in common.[36] Under simple majority rule, which is based exclusively on power in Arendt's sense and is not beholden to regulation, the danger exists that minorities may be oppressed without resort to violence—and in fact, in communities that stress consensus and the harmonization of discord, potential manifestations of pressure to conform remain a delicate matter. In my view, this is best analyzed according to the case at hand and not in general terms.

For Arendt, laws connect people, and only in the resultant space of interrelation can political power develop. A critical question becomes who issues laws and who enforces them: "It is the people's support that lends power to the institutions of a country, and this support is but the continuation of the consent that brought the laws into existence to begin with."[37]

The active support of the citizenry for an agreed-on arrangement is the precondition for obedience to the law. Moreover, laws should be directive rather than imperative, adopted rather than imposed. Where a (state) monopoly on power is absent, laws, being the rules of play for politics, make possible the free exercise of power on the part of the masses while functioning as an essential instrument to limit the abuse of power. The disregard of such laws means "the refusal to enter into the human community," and criminals place themselves outside the community that these laws constitute.[38] Violence, in contrast, compels obedience, as when a criminal uses a weapon to threaten their victim. But this obedience neither generates nor confers power.[39]

The ideal republic being a worthy goal, its vulnerability to the misuse and monopolization of power can, according to Arendt, be checked with a series of stabilizers and their structural features. Fundamental here is the idea contained in Baron Montesquieu's formulation *le pouvoir arrête le pouvoir:* "Only 'power arrests power,' that is, we must add, without destroying it, without putting impotence in the place of power."[40]

To stave off the monopolization of power, it suffices to distribute it over several planes so that power controls power and a balance of power emerges. In the polycephalic societies depicted here, the achievement of equilibrium is attributable to an array of social institutions that represent and control specific rights as well as obligations. These permit an interplay of power in combinations that maintain the society in nonhegemonic balance. Western democracies achieve a balance of power through the division of government into legislative, executive, and judicial branches. In this connection, Arendt stresses the value of positive laws, which not only stabilize but even make possible nonhegemonic life in common.[41]

A further—if asymmetrical—stabilizer for Arendt is authority, to the extent that all sides acknowledge it.[42] Thus, in ancient Rome, authority holders (senators) traditionally gave counsel to rulers without possessing executive power themselves.[43] Arendt also recognizes more recent councils that developed into institutions from self-organizing, local political organizations as well as federal societal-political structures. These allow the establishment of republics over large territories, with the possibility of expansion.[44] "Were real republics to possess these designated stabilizers, they could be considered non-hegemonic."[45]

According to the proposed reading, Arendt's concept of power signifies an elaboration and broadening of the definition of the political, and is nearly synonymous with communal action in nonhegemonic spaces. "All the properties of creativity ascribed to life in manifestations of violence and power actually belong to the faculty of action," and here the influence of violence is denied a great deal of its historical impact.

All political institutions are manifestations of power, which "petrify and decay as soon as the living power of the people ceases to uphold them."[46] One can therefore make an essential distinction between power, on the one hand, and violence and hegemony, on the other. Power requires many people; violence, because it relies on instruments, is substantially independent of the number of people. The extreme case of power is all against one; the extreme case of violence is one against all. The latter is only possible through instruments of violence. Even in a dictatorship, the individual requires myrmidons who obey his commands.

II.4. CLASTRES: THE NEUTRALIZATION OF POWER

In the 1960s and 1970s, when the French ethnologist Clastres began to engage intensively with egalitarian societies, he found that the political structures of the Indians in the Amazon region involved no coercion in the sense of "command-obedience-relations." Nonetheless, virtually all groups had authorities in the form of chiefs through whom the political became manifest. This led him to conclude that political power is universal, but a contrast must be drawn between compulsory or "coercive power" and noncompulsory, consensus-based "powerless" power.[47] From this distinction he derived the thesis that compulsion in the political realm is not the archetype of power but only a special case, viable neither as a reference point nor as an explanatory principle for its many other modalities.[48] The state, as his analysis attempts to show, cannot arise out of egalitarian political institutions. These institutions are not primitive forms of the state, and any account of the state's existence must be situated outside the history of their development within a distinct sociopolitical and historical framework.

Clastres's most significant empirical bases are his investigations into small chiefdoms where the chief possesses power, but lacks the means to carry out his will. What is the nature of such a chiefdom?

1. It is a mitigating authority. The peaceful fundament of its power is the *consensus omnium*. The chief's task is to preserve peace and harmony in the group. Outwardly he is the speaker for the group, which he represents in dealings with other groups.

2. The chief must be generous. Greed and power are incompatible.

3. The chief must be an excellent speaker. The gift of speech is both precondition and means of political power.

4. Polygyny is the exclusive privilege of the chief.[49]

The chief's speech is not intended to prompt others to take certain actions but rather is a constant injunction to internal accord and a recurrent exposition of shared values—a discourse on the community's ethos and the nature of the good. Hence, he is also the symbolic embodiment of intergroup unity. As one who constantly reiterates the cooperative ethos, the chief cannot issue orders, for such behavior would contradict his exposition of the tradition. "The chief's obligation to speak, that steady flow of empty speech that he owes the tribe, is his infinite debt, the guarantee that prevents the man of speech from becoming a man of power."[50] Through the power of his oratory, largesse, and skill at peacefully resolving conflicts, the chief accrues prestige. Prestige is a minimum of confidence on the part of the society's members that allows the execution of the integrative functions of nonhegemonic chiefs.

An essential feature of the ethnic groups examined by Clastres in the Amazon is reciprocity of exchange, but as a brake placed on power, the chief is excluded from group members' system of equal exchange. The chief must fend for himself. Exacerbating his exclusion from the principle of mutuality is the fact that he must be generous, while having fewer material goods to offer. His wives may help him make gifts, but he must craft hunting weapons and other objects considered masculine on his own. These restrictions prevent his establishing relations based on gift giving or exchange that might terminate in dependencies.

From this constellation, Clastres concludes that the essence of society and power reveals itself in the "negative correlation between asymmetry and symmetrical reciprocity."[51] The political realm is institutionalized *outside* the group and barred from gaining influence over its inner structure through the avoidance of exchange in three societally decisive spheres of circulation: goods, since the chief must give; marriage partners, because the chief alone may take multiple wives; and words, given that only the chief may speak during conflicts and represent the group to outsiders.[52] Hinrich Fink-Eitel expresses the situation thus: "Groups deny the power of the chief, which they nonetheless also demand, by excluding him from interdependent communication and holding him in a relation of powerless dependence. ... The essence of power consists in the social group's emphatic claim on something that at the same time threatens them."[53] According to Clastres, the spoken possesses special significance in this context: "By compelling the chief to move about in the area of speech alone, that is, the opposite of violence, the tribe makes certain that all things will remain in their place, that the axis of power will turn back exclusively to the social body, and that no displacement of forces will come to upset the social order."[54]

Through speech, the chief invokes an image of morality and norms that are neither decreed nor overseen by a central authority or any particular group.[55] In many societies without a state, the group ethos is engraved deeply in memory through initiation rites that are often physically and psychologically brutal; at times it is even inscribed on the body through mutilation.[56] The fact that everyone has the same marks on their body signifies, according to Clastres, that *"you will not have the desire for power; you will not have the desire for submission."*[57]

Clastres's assertions were revolutionary in their day, and many anthropologists criticized them.[58] Essential for my research is his discovery, through the example of Indian communities, that nonstate societies were successful in inhibiting coercive power. To apply his working methods to an analysis of the polycephalic societies of Ethiopia is impermissible in light of the distinct empirical bases, each of which requires its own specific methodology. In southern Ethiopia, for instance, there are no authority figures comparable to the Amazon Indian chiefs. Moreover, Clastres's thesis that the conscious avoidance of coercive power is only achievable in small, manageable societies is shown to be invalid here.[59] Yet there are correspondences in the ways that power is used to achieve consensus and social peace in both small Indian groups and the populous polycephalic societies of southern Ethiopia. The strength of the ethos as expressed in legal conceptions offers a departure point for the present investigation. Jürgen Habermas's theoretical contributions concerning communicative action and discourse ethics, which will be examined in the next section, provide suggestions for analysis.

My own considerations and those of Clastres overlap in our reflections on our own societies. Those who view statelessness as something other than a shortcoming, who take up the theme of stateless societies—or more strictly, societies that maintain as great a distance as possible between themselves and the paternalism of the state—will inevitably be led to critically examine their own societal models, which incorporate the state monopoly on violence.

II.5. HABERMAS: COMMUNICATIVE ACTION AND THE ESTABLISHMENT OF NORMS

Foucault and Arendt draw a line between power, on the one hand, and violence and misuse of power, on the other, and emphasize the productive and creative potential of the first. For Arendt, all communitarian action is potentially societal power. But whose hands does this action lie in, and what factors set it in motion? How does the potential power of a given society come to be deployed for nonviolent, productive conviviality, and how does it counteract violence and the misuse of power? In response, Arendt posits nonviolent communicative power. And Habermas has developed a theoretically grounded approach to the ways that communicative action might be organized and implemented in society.

For the polycephalic societies under examination here, the discussion must begin with the prescriptive validity of those moral sentiments and norms that have not hardened into merely rehearsed conventions but instead are validated through their correspondence with the perspectives of a society's members along with their expression of behavioral expectations and disapproval. Habermas proceeds from the notion that when a society reflects on the value of normative propositions, participants will assess these to be justified, confirmed, or unjustified.[60] Though law, morality, and norms differ, they are closely linked semantically, so that normative propositions, when legitimated through the process of reflection, show themselves as suitable guidelines for laws. The demand for a discussion process of this type is evident in the speech that opens deliberations in southern Ethiopia: "We, who are ever obliged to the good, we who ever avoid the bad, we discuss in common how we should shape our life together."[61]

In his *Theory of Communicative Action*, Habermas brings together communication and action theory into a new, philosophically grounded social scientific model. Communicative action here signifies "a type of interaction that is *coordinated through* speech acts and does not *coincide with* them."[62] Language is instrumental here as a medium in which communication partners negotiate their affairs so that understanding-oriented coordinated action can be possible. Since expressions of opinion can be pure "egocentric calculations of utility," Habermas separates the strategic action of individuals from societal, understanding-oriented communicative action. Communication is social action to the degree that it is based on "cooperative processes of interpretation," and the rationality of social action is established through nonrepressive forms of communication. Consensus must be achieved under conditions of "communicative rationality"—that is, in confrontation with disputable arguments in a nonhegemonic forum.[63]

Such communication demands that individuals recognize the subjectivity of their perceptions and relativize them in their confrontation with other "actors," thereby in principle permitting their submission to rational critique. Justifiable arguments asserted by coequal peers should form the basis for consensus on the validity of their expressions and subsequent understanding-oriented coordinated action.[64] The basis of such an action model, in which "participants in interaction can now mobilize the rationality potential ... expressly for the cooperatively pursued goal of reaching understanding," is a shared, intersubjective lifeworld that "stores the interpretive work of preceding generations." This forms the background against which situations are interpreted and the struggle for the validation of norms takes place.[65]

Formal and Rational Criteria of Argumentation

In order to guarantee equality of opportunity for participants, Habermas formulates generally binding formal rules:

all subjects capable of speech and action may take part in discussion, but only to assert their own beliefs. They are not to contradict themselves, and they have the right to both interrogate any assertion and insert any assertion into the discourse. Only under these conditions is equal participation in communicative exchange possible.[66] At the discussion's end, validity is accorded only to that which *all* participants have agreed on.[67] Consensus cannot depend on momentary or alleged certitudes but rather must take *rationally* motivated accord as its basis. This rationality, which is of central importance for Habermas, is only attainable through language. Thus, for Habermas, to be rational, a norm "must satisfy the condition that the consequences and side effects its general observance can be anticipated to have for the satisfaction of the interests of each could be freely accepted by all affected."[68] This can only apply for norms that "regulate problems of communal life in the common interest and thus are 'equally good' for all affected." If we have agreed to norms governing rational arguments and all conversation partners recognize the balanced nature of the judgment, then we may feel ourselves duty bound to them. Such duties, according to Habermas, constrain the will, but protect the autonomy of subjects in that they are the pure result of their rational activity.

Meaning and Application Discourse

As the rationality of norms depends on the acceptance of their consequences and secondary effects, their claims to validity are indexed by time and knowledge: norms reflect the state of knowledge with all available information.[69]

Habermas distinguishes, on the one hand, meaning discourses derived from universalism (which flow into general norms), and on the other hand, application discourses suited to a given case, which take the realities of the lifeworld into consideration and make understanding between human beings possible.[70] So that the "pure types of linguistically mediated interaction can be brought progressively closer to the complexity of natural situations," Habermas advocates "reversing step by step the strong idealizations by which we have built up the concept of communicative action," and including, along with understanding processes and communicative action, "the resources of the background knowledge from which participants feed their interpretations."[71]

The more a subject's inhabited lifeworld plays a role in the management of problems, the more the overarching discourse community differentiates itself into subcommunities. These are not forums for universalizing meaning discourses but rather for application discourses concerned with issues that may arise. There is no guarantee that the latter will achieve universal validity. And yet Habermas proposes that we do consider this as a goal of inquiry, because in a society united by consensus, even if all participants voice their respective arguments, the danger remains that falsehood may attain legitimacy. Here, a frankly unsettling thought experiment of Zygmunt Bauman's (with no relation to Habermas) demonstrates the normative strength of what has been transformed into fact. In his critical remarks on the negotiability of morality, Bauman writes, "In the case of a victory of the Germans, the crimes of the National Socialists would have entered into the textbooks as the history of human progress."[72]

In both application and meaning discourses, the life-world aids orientation when norms come into conflict. "It is the conservative counterweight to the risk of disagreement that arises with every actual process of reaching under-standing."[73] The lifeworld forms the basis for all communi-cation. It cannot be questioned in its entirety because to do so would signify the liquidation of a society and disappear-ance of its culture. Individual facets, however, remain grasp-able in theory and amenable to inquiry.

Reference to the lifeworld contributes to the adequacy of the solutions encountered in relation to conflicts between norms in nonhegemonic discourse. But these must also cohere with extant norms and form a meaningful system of rules.[74] If established rules take into account social and col-lective ends while offering the individual space for develop-ment, then the question of the reasonableness of norms and regulations moves into the foreground. The solution to this problem, according to Habermas, "motivates the transition from morality to law."[75]

In line with his basic evolutionary orientation, Haber-mas seems to view positive law as a necessary corollary of the pluralization of life-forms, whereas in "small and rela-tively undifferentiated groups" it is possible to regulate behavior through the embedding of communicative action in the lifeworld.[76] In any case, for him, the function of law extends beyond the mere regulation of conduct and forms "the medium of social integration."[77] Ethnological case studies, however, confirm that in polycephalic societies, generally accepted law is elaborated discursively. Habermas invokes Arendt's concept of *communicative power*, which mobilizes the communicative power of the citizenry and in turn makes possible the production of legitimate law. It is a power that "manifests itself in orders that protect political liberty; in resistance against the forms of repression that threaten political liberty internally or externally."[78] As soon as a society cedes its unrestricted freedom of action to a state authority, it loses this freedom. "The more the bonding force of communicative action wanes in private life spheres and the embers of communicative freedom die out, the easier it is for someone who monopolizes the public sphere to align the mutually estranged and isolated actors into a mass that can be directed and mobilized."[79]

For our observations, Habermas's conception exhibits the following core tenet: social actions are verbally mediated. In noncoercive communication between individuals, convictions arise from reasonably debatable arguments that all members of the community deem acceptable. In communicative action, novel situations are problematized and rendered intelligible through concepts. Against the background of the individual worldview, discussion participants apprehend new complexes of meaning and make discoveries together so that they may arrive at suitable understanding-oriented coordinated action. Hence, a community-forming vigor permeates discourses about value and the positing of moral problems as realized in nonhegemonic reflection. Together with institutions built up in common, this discourse affords its participants a power that remains operational so long as it is kept alive through communicative action. This power potentially counteracts the misuse or monopolization of power, and offers opportunities for resistance or the undermining of external hegemonic influences and claims to domination.

If one keeps in mind that polycephalic societies are hardly so undifferentiated as Habermas supposes, and that their conception of the law extends far past the societally stabilizing function that the common lifeworld demands, then his considerations offer valuable suggestions for ethnological research.

Universalism

Especially since the Enlightenment, many occidental thinkers have attempted to formulate and justify universally valid principles for ethical questions. Habermas too aims to satisfy a universal claim to moral validity and thus arrive at lasting global principles. His discourse ethics rely explicitly on the universalistic ethics of Kant along with their dialectical linkage between free will and reason. Habermas attempts to concretize Kant's abstract ethics and apply them to societal processes.[80]

Habermas considers universal validity claims necessary in modern societies because they "detach themselves from the concrete contents of the plurality of attitudes toward life that now manifest themselves." He adds that "a morality that rests only on the normative content of universal conditions of coexistence in a society ... [and] in general must be universalistic and egalitarian in respect of the validity and sphere of application of its norms; at the same time, it is formal and empty in the content of its norms."[81]

Nevertheless, the claim to universality runs into two problems:

1. It is to the merit, above all, of ethnology to have documented how, in different parts of the world, moral norms and the configuration of ethical problems are bound up with specific interpretations of the world. While it is true that people in all known societies deliberate on which behaviors are proper to and essential for life in common, the results of such deliberations may be widely divergent, and yet sensible and "rational" in their respective contexts. Annette Hornbacher has shown that in order to satisfy a claim to universality, either a world ethos (Hans Küng) or cosmopolitan ethos (Paul Rabinow) is required, although both cannot exist at the same time.[82]

Habermas raises no claim to totality, and his considerations take account of specific world interpretations in application discourse. But his primary concern remains the establishment of a morality with links to history and the lifeworld. The norms that eventuate from such an undertaking, he believes, could lay claim to universal validity. I'll leave that "could" in the conditional.

2. Habermas's conception of reason and rationality places a restriction on his model. Both concepts imply notions

of progressively higher development. Unlike the majority of his colleagues in the field, he does take his observations beyond European intellectual history and even draws examples from ethnology. Following the evolutionary conception—which one would like to think has been long refuted—Habermas depicts "traditional" societies outside Europe as archaic forerunners of our developed societies, as if the lineaments of our prehistory were visible in their history and present reality, and in doing so, he overlooks their contemporary character.[83] Even if he does not dispute other societies' cognitive capacities or the logical structure of their thinking, his image of them still suggests an archaic approach to life. Drawing on the work of Claude Lévi-Strauss and Maurice Godelier, he concludes that the "worldview structures" corresponding to the "mythic way of understanding the world" are not by nature reflective and "do not allow action orientations that might be called rational by the implicit standards of today."[84] Consequently, only *we* (in industrialized Western countries) are suited to the rational way of life. Habermas thus discards Peter Winch's 1970 thesis that "in every linguistically articulated worldview and every cultural form of life there is an incommensurable concept of rationality."[85] In an earlier study, Hornbacher emphasized, in contrast to Habermas, the reflective potential of mythical traditions, and in her research on Bali, she has made clear their potential for generating creative knowledge processes.[86]

The unquestioned presumption of the superiority of occidental rationality and its concomitant claim to universality prohibits the direct application of Habermas's theoretical considerations on communicative procedure to societies that have not been "illuminated" by the Enlightenment. If I question this claim to universality, I break with an essential component of his model. But it is possible to modify certain of Habermas's arguments provided that we approach them from another perspective. My ethnological research has shown that a stable system of reasoning is characteristic of societies untouched by the Enlightenment, and that there, too, claims to legitimacy are assayed through rational, nonhegemonic, community-centered discourse—the very benchmarks that the theory of communicative action demands. To this extent, the expanded concept of rationality that these case studies reveal offers a reasonable analogy to Habermas's theses, and they in turn provide a platform for consideration of my own analysis. This is particularly true when anthropologists confront societies in which decisions and the interpretation of situations are explored and dealt with through argumentation among individuals endowed with equal rights.

Attributes: The Relation between Subject and Collective

It is a widespread, Eurocentric presumption that in "traditional" societies, the individual develops in the context of a collective we and is only capable of free decision making in limited circumstances. Naturally, Habermas's view is not quite so unsophisticated. To quote his paraphrase of (the late) Ernst Tugendhat, "My understanding of myself as a person is interwoven with my social identity in such a way that I can value myself only if the community of which I view myself as a part and whose authority is binding for me confirms me in my status as a member."[87] Still, for Habermas, the collective interrelatedness of the members of traditional societies sharing a "mythical understanding of the world" constitutes a drawback because "in traditional societies, moral norms are indeed so closely bound up with religious worldviews and shared forms of life that individuals learn what it means to enjoy the status of membership in a community thus founded through identification with the contents of this established concrete ethical life."[88]

It is not clear to me which "traditional societies" Habermas believes he has described here. His assessment does not hold true for the societies I examine, which are definitely not "modern" and are deeply rooted in tradition. In the polycephalic societies of southern Ethiopia, the concept of the person is bound with the notion of the soul and this in its turn is closely bound to the notion of the individual self.[89]

This conception dictates that a person is healthy and capable of action when embedded in the larger context of the community as an autonomous being, responsible to self, peers, ancestors, and the unborn. Grown people belong to various social fields or institutions with partly opposed interests, and are considered competent for action when the independent decisions that they make are seen as rational within this societal framework. According to my observations among the Burji-Konso Cluster, the semantic field that I call "rational" relates inevitably to the following:

knowledge, understanding, and wisdom; intelligence; and truthfulness and responsibility.

The resulting consciousness is a *tertium comparationis* of personalities and traditional values. Here, personal capacities, character traits, and notions passed down from elders about the proper form of life (though obviously utterly distinct from the occidental concept of the individual) come together. This kind of consciousness may not be called self-reflective, but it does rest on experience, especially the recognition that one's well-being is made possible through the well-being of others. This is something distinct from ethics as "customary morality."

III POWER, LAW, AND NONHEGEMONY IN POLYCEPHALIC SOCIETIES IN THE HORN OF AFRICA

Power relations—as has been stated—are an attribute of human life in common, and appear in numerous shapes and modalities, among which coercive power is merely a possible form and not at all a telos toward which power relations inevitably tend, however frequent this propensity may be. A determinant factor in the direction of their development is the nature of discourses on power in a given society and the historical circumstances that have led to the empirically observable situation. In the societies I examine, which reject the elevation of one person over another, communication plays a key role among members endowed with equal rights, either because this communication was *at one time* successful and its results passed down interpretatively, or because it is an unvarying feature.

The question of which factors have contributed to egalitarian behavior in southern Ethiopian polycephalic societies and why central authority has not arisen from it remains open. Undoubtedly the above-described interlinked institutions have played a crucial part, even if they have undergone changes in their recent history, such as urbanization and the growth of the diaspora. Particular importance lies both with the historical, political, and economic processes that attack these structures, and the norm and value conceptions that insulate them. A critical question is to what extent the legal conceptions that have emerged from the positing of certain norms safeguard institutions and help restrain coercive power.

But what are the foremost dangers that engender paternalism and hegemony in these social orders that have been passed on to the present day, and to what degree does law aid in warding them off? The history of the Horn of Africa shows that heritable clan or lineage chief positions can transform their socioreligious power into political power, and that elected dignitaries may expand their domains or attempt to assign their functions exclusively to themselves and their heirs. In some areas, Big Men also seek to expand their influence. Moreover, different parties striving for dominance may rise up during internal conflicts and attempt to cultivate a devoted clientele.

Pressure from without by state authorities as well as, for just over two decades, the aggressive proselytizing of US evangelical sects threaten to subvert egalitarian values. Sects assert the unequivocal truth of the Christian teachings that they promote, and in doing so, put indigenous values, morals, and legal conceptions in the wrong. This makes of *truth* a warrant for hegemony, instrumentalized through strict sanctions directed against any indigenous religious practice, in the full knowledge that in these societies, religious and social practice are indivisible.

III.1. SIGNIFICANT PERSONS

What dangers in polycephalic societies permit hegemonic ambitions to threaten their ability to function, and how are these dangers confronted? To answer this question, it is first necessary to take a closer look at political and religious dignitaries.

III.1.1. *Regulus Sacer*

The heads of clans and lineages symbolize the unity of patrilineal kinship bonds, and even today, when officially they embrace Ethiopian Orthodox Christianity, they continue to fulfill sacred functions from traditional religion. The authority and spiritual power assigned to the *qaalluu* of the Borana (Oromo), *qawot* of the Arbore (Hoor), *ganni* of the Burji, *dhaama* of the Dirashe and Mosiye, *poqolho* of the Dullay, *ka'o* of the Gamo, and *poqalla* of the Konso must be used for the good of the community. The supreme chiefs who often wield political influence today descend from these groups. Elsewhere in Ethiopia, they were the breeding ground for erstwhile sacred rulers and state founding fathers.

But among the Oromo, where a Gada system prevails, the importance of clan or lineage heads is limited. The reason lies with the dual organization of Oromo society, which was originally split into two exogamous halves or moieties. During the sixteenth- and seventeenth-century Oromo migrations, which reached as far as Tigray to the north and deep into present-day Kenya to the south, this dual organization was passed down to the individual migrant groups, of which the Borana are one of the largest. The leaders of the Borana moieties, known as qaalluu, are considered the most important spiritual leaders.[1] They incarnate the divine sources of human order, mediate between people and the supernatural, celebrate important rituals essential for fertility, welfare, prosperity, and law, and give a feeling of unity to the far-flung population. Moreover, they fulfill ritual functions in the Gada system, though their relationship to it is in some ways antagonistic. The qaalluu must stand above party politics, may not bear arms, and may not kill. In the imperial era, after colonization, some from their ranks were named *balabats*, thus cementing their influence until the 1974 revolution.

In the Gamo Highlands, which flank the East African Rift Valley to the south, the majority of Ometo-speaking ethnic groups possess no centralized political authority either; instead, politics takes place in the people's assembly. And yet despite a number of similarities, the social structure of the ethnic subgroups or *dere* is not at all uniform, and the socioreligious significance of lineage and clan elders evinces a wide spectrum of variation.[2] In contrast to their Cushitic-speaking neighbors with ties to the "democratic" Gada system, the erstwhile-sacred kingdoms continue to hold influence among Omotic speakers. Within the *dere*, there is a hierarchy of *reguli sacri* with the ka'o at the head. His religious capacities and obligations coincide in essence with what is said about reguli sacri elsewhere in this chapter, but he is also considered the "eldest" of the "community" and territory, and this has tempted some anthropologists into viewing him as a king.[3] As the steward of traditional rules to which he himself is subject, he is indispensable to society's well-being. He also plays an important role in assuring that arrangements with neighboring groups are honored. Throughout history, there have always been ka'o who wished to broaden their power base. Their official incorporation as chiefs into the imperial administration only worsened this tendency.

Among the ethnic groups of the Burji-Konso Cluster, the spectrum of clan and lineage elders ranges from relatively insignificant sacrificial priests to influential dignitaries reminiscent of a sacred kingdom, although there is less diversity than in the Gamo Highlands. The important clan and lineage elders of the Burji-Konso Cluster trace their origins to first ancestors who, according to myth, were born of the lakes, calabash fruits, or serpents. These ancestors passed down special powers, religious insignia, and cultural possessions to them. As a link between the living and their forbears, they guarantee fertility and order, and are a symbol of life.[4] But invoking their heritage alone is not sufficient to establish legitimacy; only when they fulfill their obligations do they show themselves worthy of their position. Their essential task consists in employing their spiritual powers for the good of the people by warding off drought, field vermin, epidemics, and other plagues. They bless seeds, lead ceremonies for the first harvest, and bless those newly initiated into the Gada system, thereby ensuring the flow of life. They must observe dietary restrictions and taboos, may not engage in physical labor, may not touch the ground with a hoe, and may only leave their group's settlement under strict conditions. Most clan and lineage elders may only kill during sacrifices, and they themselves may not be killed, even in the event of war. They may offer their farmstead as a haven to members of their ethnic group guilty of killing until the aggrieved parties have come to an amicable solution through the responsible forums.

Alongside their power to bless, many clan and lineage elders possess a destructive capacity that may be employed in compensatory ways to preserve human and cosmic order. They may use it to withhold their fertility-granting blessing from the society. It also enables them to intervene in rivalries among peers or oppose the generational groups. Their spiritual potency marks them out as dangerous; hence, in Konso, the poqalla live not in the walled towns but rather on hills between the settlements. In the past, this meant, among other things, that they could act as a peacemakers during conflicts between towns, and even today, they arbitrate in feuds between localities over land use or water rights.[5] In addition to peacemaking, their powers have made it possible for them—and not only in the past—to integrate spiritual functions into strategies of political power.[6]

Lineage elders in southern Ethiopia hold not only high religious and social status but in some cases have obtained great wealth during specific historical events. I can retrace this phenomenon among the southern Dullay. Their tradition dictates that the poqolho offer protection to the persecuted and needy on their farmsteads, and in return, these people work the fields of the reguli sacri. When imperial northern Ethiopia took over these settlements, the poqolho became responsible for the drastically increasing numbers of widows and orphans as well as those impoverished through plunder. Initially, this clientele was an economic burden for the lineage elders, but with time, their combined manpower became a great advantage over other farmers, who were forced to perform drudge work for the Amharic occupiers and could no longer maintain the cooperative labor systems that the agricultural economy required. Lineage elders also managed to multiply their landholdings through special entitlements concerning the redistribution of lands lacking hereditary claims. There are, however, systematic restrictions that impinge on these entitlements. "Landholdings" consist in essence of field lands, which belong to the lineage, and which the lineage elder manages as a kind of trustee. As the authority responsible for the allocation of these lands, the lineage elder can reserve an outsize portion for himself. But his affluence is bound by an indissoluble obligation: lineage elders must care for members of their lineage who have fallen into need. To supply the needy with seeds is not charity but instead a duty.

Clan and lineage elders possess high status, are often affluent, and enjoy significant powers—but competing institutions and sanctions curb any potential ambition for employing these for political or economic gain.[7] Nor do these dignitaries possess command authority, as is clear from the story of a poqalla named Kalla in Konso. When a prominent regulus sacer died in 2003 and the time came for his successor's inauguration, the ceremonial preparations broke off because the clan and ritual assistants repeatedly failed to supply the required sacrificial bulls. Harsh words, even from the *poqalteta*—the first wife of the deceased poqalla—did not help, and the chosen aspirant to the poqalla could not straighten things out either. With matters at a standstill, an elder advised the designated successor that "you must listen better to the people." Obviously he took this advice, since in the end the ceremony occurred.[8]

Yet even if these dignitaries are generally responsible for their own lineage and only rarely for their clans, and their ambitions are subject to limitations, it is still possible for a minority to use its spiritual powers to prevail over others and extend its sphere of influence, as with the qaalluu of the Borana, beyond the kinship group and over a larger settlement community. In many of the Dullay ethnic groups, lineage elders have weakened their rivals and imposed themselves as regional regulus sacer.[9] The oral traditions of the Burji, however, relate that at an assembly of various clans, they chose a ganni as their regulus sacer. His spiritual position was higher than that of the customary lineage elder (*gosand ana*), and with time the office and title became heritable in the patrilineal line. The dhaama of the Dirashe had power over the rain and could grant fertility. Honored far beyond the Dirashe's realm, he was the most important regulus sacer of the entire Burji-Konso Cluster. In 1975, the revolutionary guard divested him of power and drove him out of his homeland.

The influence as well as status of clan and lineage elders were and are dependent on external developments. After the conquest of the south, the regime instituted the post of administrative chief (balabat) in accordance with the principle of indirect rule. Hereditary clan and lineage heads appeared best suited to this role, and attained a new political status.[10] Their spiritual position remained more or less intact, as the conquerors held their missionary zeal in check. After the 1974 Ethiopian Revolution, when the post of balabat was abolished, these political powers were revoked, and holders of the post were generally expelled, with the people—often rightly—reproaching them for having enriched themselves during the imperial period. Clan and lineage elders also lost their religious rank and spiritual powers, because the Revolutionary Guard (zemecha) that was sent out to the countryside discriminated far more harshly against the indigenous religions than against Christianity, and following the example of the Chinese Cultural Revolution, frequently destroyed the regalia of religious dignitaries. After the victory of the present regime in 1991, religion and religious life experienced a resurgence all over Ethiopia. While indigenous priests and the regulus sacer were once more embraced, it became clear that basic religious patterns had persisted in the society—and indeed, continue to exist.[11]

III.1.2.   Additional Socially Influential Persons

Polycephalic societies in southern Ethiopia invariably exhibit a tendency toward a dual separation of power into complementary religious and secular domains. But this separation is not absolute, for the reguli sacri described above also act in the secular domain, and dignitaries responsible for day-to-day administration and political affairs frequently perform religious obligations.

This holds true as well for Big Men (see section I.2), who acquire influence and power through wealth or heroic deeds in battle, and at times use their position despotically. This was common in the formerly polycephalic Oromo groups to the west of Addis Ababa and further south in the Gibe region (see below), but occurred only seldom in the polycephalic societies of southern Ethiopia.[12] There, alongside hereditary lineage elders, dignitaries charged with political tasks were elected for a limited term, and only rarely for life.[13] Potential candidates are frequently monitored for years to assess their fitness and character, and special care is taken to see that they are disinclined to imperiousness.[14]

Still, ambitious dignitaries have tried to expand their power and extend their reign beyond their elected period. Even today, they often strive to pass their post down to their offspring. The concept of "inheritance" must be used here with caution. It comes from our culture and is misleading unless we clarify how the ethnic group under consideration understands it in a given situation. Though anthropologists do speak of "inheritance" in certain cases, for these societies it is neither normatively regulated, as we have seen with the lineage elders, nor compulsory. It is, however, possible that it has developed in the course of their history.

Candidates for a position are often chosen from the same clan or lineage, with certain kinship groups accorded special powers for giving blessings. A person responsible for rain ceremonies will be chosen from a family line thought to possess a special relationship to the rain. A candidate from this group will see his chances improve if his father or grandfather served in this same capacity to the community's satisfaction—making him a promising prospect for this important duty.[15] But if in the course of his duties, a dignitary responsible for rain has struggled with crop failures or has quarrelsome sons, the position will go to another person from a different line, thus breaking the hereditary chain.

In the Konso cities, a specific kind of heredity is associated with the post of *aappa timpaa* (father of the drum), which plays an important role in their legal system. The post and drum circulate among a number of predetermined lineages, and the keeper of the drum will be chosen, depending on the region, for a term of two or three years. The drum (*timpaa*) symbolizes the inner cohesion of the society, inner peace, and law and order.[16]

Other forms of inheritance that arise may pose a grave danger of undermining the polycephalic social order. Among the Dullay-speaking ethnic groups, after the collapse of the Gada system in the early twentieth century, the office of speaker (*hayyo*), which originally expired along with the Gada ranking associated with it, became heritable. Still, the hayyo's sphere of activity is highly limited, and if he carries out his functions poorly, a new one can be chosen to take his place.[17]

Graver developments took place among the political functionaries of the Burji, originally elected on a temporary basis, occasionally among the Gamo peoples and possibly among the Borana as well. The threat elected officials represented for the continuity of polycephalic societies is evident in historical events in the Gibe region to the north of Kaffa. There, elected Oromo dignitaries brought the egalitarian system to collapse. Within decades, the Gada system gave way to elected military leaders who rose to the position of despots.[18]

State authorities in the imperial era hardly paid attention to indigenous offices, but after 1975, the Derg regime either prohibited these title bearers or subjected them to pressure. Such dignitaries still existed, though, during my visits to Konso in 1981 and 1984, at least to an extent and in certain places, and after the overthrow of the Derg, they experienced a degree of revival.

In the Burji-Konso Cluster, elected political functionaries whose competencies extended beyond clan, region, and generation groups only existed among the Burji: the *woma* for the southern Burji, and *dayna* for those in the north. Whoever sought these posts, which entailed political duties and ritual obligations, had to assure the well-being of the population with generous feasts and gifts. For outside observers, these two dignitaries looked like chiefs, but they were subordinate to the dictates of the great council, and at first their term lasted only one year.[19] In conformity with the reigning dual order in southern Ethiopia, they fulfilled reciprocal duties and were dependent on one another. During the inauguration, for example, each had to consent to the other's appointment.

Rivalries arose frequently between woma and dayna, at times degenerating into blood feuds. The frontier situation around 1900 made it possible for one woma to expand his political influence considerably, and his successors extended their mandate and eventually came to occupy the post for life. As with lineage elders elsewhere, woma and dayna were integrated into the northern Ethiopian administrative system until the revolution did away with the positions. Years-long discussions about reinstituting it, and who would be worthy to serve, are examined further below.

III.2. DEMARCATION AND CONTROL OF THE COMPETENCIES OF DIGNITARIES

In southern Ethiopia, lineage elders and the authorities who have emerged from their ranks possess significant authority. But there existed, and continue to exist, social control mechanisms that ensure obedience to reigning norms. The spiritual authority of the reguli sacri is beyond appeal, but ritual practices often place limits on their autonomy. This is particularly true for lineage elders whose influence and sphere of activity extend past their own lineage.

Even in authoritarian, formerly sacred kingdoms, rulers were overseen by an institution described in the literature as a state council. An example is the rigidly sacred kingdom of Yem, some 150 miles to the south of Addis Ababa. There the king was lord over life and death, and had the power to impose terrible punishments. But if he failed in his duties or was guilty of malfeasance, the state council could condemn him to death in turn.[20] In polycephalic societies, assemblies watched over and debated the conduct of lineage elders and other officials.

In the Dullay language region and among the Dirashe, where the high reguli sacri are comparable to priestly chiefs, sacrificial rites require an officiator known as the *haalho/ohado*. The Dullay origin myths describe the mythical ancestor of the haalho as the older brother of the poqolho, who in accordance with the rule of seniority bears the exclusive right to slaughter sacrificial offerings. Interestingly, the haalho must come from the circle of craftsmen (*hawdo*); this restricts the power of the priestly chiefs to members of a collective who constitute a minority within the agricultural population.

Along with officiants, lineage elders require a first wife as a helpmate, and she alone is allowed to prepare certain sacrificial offerings.[21] The people's assembly chooses this first wife, and in this way, retains an important influence on the regulus sacer's behavior. They can delay his investiture until agreement is reached.

High lineage elders were prohibited from killing and hence could not become warlords; this constrained their possible authority to give orders. Despite this regulation, authoritarian religious kingdoms did arise. Therefore a leader must not take direct part in struggles.

Complementary Opposition: The Gada System

The most effective counterpower to the regulus sacer is the Gada system with its democratic basic structure. Though it does not preclude leader personalities, it appears to control them effectively. Among the Borana, the elected high chiefs of the Gada and qaalluu, as the most important religious leaders, must avoid one another for the length of their terms except in certain established rituals.[22] This avoidance comes with a proviso: the Gada and their leaders offer political as well as economic security to the qaalluu, and they in turn require the qaalluu's blessing at their appointment. Spiritual and military leaders, the latter with a limited term of office, thus depend on and oversee one another so that neither group becomes too powerful. For this reason, Asmarom Legesse concludes that the Oromo spread power across generations and institutions better than Western democracies, producing balanced opposition instead of hierarchies.[23]

Complementary opposition between generation groups with egalitarian principles and the authority of the reguli sacri, which represents a hereditarily legitimated institution, also exists in Konso. The social and political influence of the venerated poqalla is limited by the body of elders in the Gada system as well as the demands of the territorial groups with their elected councils of elders. In return, every new generation group requires the blessing of a poqalla, and the tree planted at a cult site (mooraa) as a symbol of unity during Gada transition ceremonies must come from the sacred grove of one of the great poqalla.

Even in regions of southern Ethiopia where only vestiges of the Gada system remain, it has left its mark on the Dullay value system. There, the poqolho originally stood in a complementary relationship to the Gada system. Both institutions had social, territorial, and religious duties and obligations, but clear separations hindered power imbalances. Assemblies were responsible for direct political decisions, and they excluded the poqolho's participation. Moreover, the latter's spiritual role disallowed them from cultivating land, making them dependent on the population, and therefore on members of the Gada system. Yet the Gada system was separable neither from the religious conceptions nor worldview of the Dullay culture, and it bound the living to past and future generations as well as assuring the biological and spiritual continuity of the community. Dignitaries from the Gada system could only exercise their position with the blessing of the poqolho, though he had no role of his own in Gada ceremonies. These two power domains held one another in a tense, antagonistic balance, and this equilibrium was perceived as ideal. With the decline of the Gada system at the end of the nineteenth century, the power of the reguli sacri grew. This does not mean that they acquired a monopoly on power; even without the Gada system, elders' assemblies ensured that religious dignitaries remained scrupulous in the fulfillment of their duties. In the end, while this is a question of religious principles and obligations, it still possesses a legal character. The narrowness of the bonds linking these domains is clear from the fact that the same overarching term encompasses such obligations, norms, and laws.

A regulus sacer stands outside the Gada system and is at times even excluded from legal proceedings. The story from Gollango told at the beginning of this book reports how the lineage head's prerogative of issuing legal verdicts passed over to a council that forbade his participation, and his role was reduced to ratifying its verdicts. The lineage head's monopoly on violence was broken "democratically" and this removed the danger of the elder's transforming his role into a centralized authority.

The majority of Dullay neighboring groups in the Gamo Highlands are structured according to clear differences in rank, but exhibit no centralized authority. Instead, authority is distributed among three carefully balanced institutional groups—assemblies, priests, and dignitaries—each with its respective tasks and rights: while reguli sacri are responsible for the religious and ritual life of the community, political concerns rest in the hands of the assembly and its representatives, the *halaqa*, whom the people's assembly elects for a limited period of time.[24] Their post accords them certain privileges that come with obligations. To prevent them from accruing coercive power, before the vote, two halaqa are selected to compete politically and economically. To win the population's approval, they throw enormous feasts that garner great prestige but also often ruin them economically. Yet the high esteem that they are held in does not bring with it the authority to give orders, and they occupy no permanent leadership position. One halaqa who strove immoderately for power was sent into eternal exile.[25]

"Democratic" and "monarchical" ideologies long coexisted in the Gamo Highland, with implementation oscillating between these two poles, so that ethnic groups there "have been described both as small kingdoms and small republics."[26] This shows the many ways that different ethnic groups configure the spatial and temporal crossovers between the hegemonic institutions of the sacred kingdom and regulus sacer, who was bound exclusively to the religious realm.

Sanctions

What sanctions may the community impose if a regulus sacer shows himself unworthy of his post? A widely told tale in southern Ethiopia about an arrogant regulus sacer acting like a king who gave the population tasks that were impossible to fulfill (for example, to bring forth a cow that urinated milk) gives an indication.[27]

A version of this story was recorded in Konso in the 1930s, and similar versions exist among the Dullay and Dirashe. In the end, the elected leaders of the Gada system intervene: "At that the *Heijus* assembled all the people and they resolved to kill the king [the poqalla]. They dug a deep pit and laid an ox pelt atop it. Men sat around the edges of the pit to hold it in place. The *Heijus* invited the king to come. ... The king came and sat on the pelt. The men stood up, and the king fell in the pit. The *Heijus* said: 'You did not leave the people in peace, now you will die in this pit.' They threw earth upon him until the pit was full."[28]

In the conflict between the community, as represented by the elders, and the tyrannical regulus sacer, the community comes out on top. The intelligence of the elders and their council overcomes coercive power. They do not abolish the position of regulus sacer but instead send a clear signal to such future dignitaries not to misuse their position. In most versions of the tale, the population takes an active role by determining the new officeholder.

Should inexplicable misfortunes (droughts and the like) occur in the territory and prosperity fail to appear, suspicion will soon fall on presumed dereliction by one of the lineage elders responsible for fertility and the community's well-being. This will require a meeting of the councils assigned to legal questions, which will examine these suspicions, and if they are found to be true, discuss possible sanctions. Unlike in other cases, where the infractor is present, this will happen in the lineage elder's absence. If his offense is deemed substantiated, chosen elders will convey a warning to him. If this is ineffective, the responsible council may decide to impose a fine, strip him of his political powers, or ostracize or banish him.

Our dialogue partners in Burji described this plainly. If despite the warning, prosperity did not come, the southern Burji would drive all ganni from their farms to a district to the south of Burji town, where they would stay for perhaps a week in huts without provisions. If the hungry ganni were set free, they would promise from then on to give their blessing for a good harvest. A conciliation ritual followed, and the community gave reparations for any damages incurred.

There have been graver consequences. Burji tradition explains that before the Amharic conquest, religious dignitaries who used their power over the rain to the community's detriment could be sentenced to death. The last-reported execution took place at the end of the nineteenth century— by strangulation, as misfortune could come to the land if the ganni's blood touched the ground.[29]

I was told of further sanctions in the Dullay region and Dirashe. After the revolution in Konso, the regulus sacer Bamalle was accused of striving for power, and his farm was set on fire. When his hidden store of hand grenades and ammunition exploded, it destroyed his entire property. The father of this important poqalla had also nurtured great ambitions for leadership. He had once hoped that the Italian invaders would appoint him "head chief over all of Konso."[30]

Similar factors are likely at play in the unusual death of a ganni from Burji. Before his appointment, he had led an easy life as a well-off long-haul trucker. After being named ganni, he struggled to fulfill the hopes placed in him, and his engagement in partisan politics met with disapproval. He was declared an outcast (c'urd'a) in the mid-1990s. As a friend from Marsabit wrote to me in May 1998, "The truth is, many were irritated by his unofficial trips. His behavior was unworthy (of his post). He lapsed in his obligation to oversee the community's well-being. In Nairobi, he had a stomach problem. He decided to use traditional herbs. He died from an overdose."

Community measures in response to transgressions of values are undoubtedly harsher for dignitaries than for people who hold no official position. This is particularly true for hereditary lineage elders whose public position of socioreligious power best situates them to pursue their interests to the detriment of their society's calibrated harmony. In extreme cases, this has led to the imposition of the death penalty, otherwise unknown in these societies, where in general the most severe punishment is banishment—and even that is subject to repeal.

Striving for Hegemony among Reguli Sacri

Even in polycephalic societies, lineage elders and others of comparable status repeatedly try to employ their spiritual offices to attain political power. The community watches closely over such inclinations, and it is no coincidence that during the inauguration ceremony for a ganni, the women in Burji sing a song admonishing him to uphold the separation of political and religious duties. Polycephalic ethnic groups are also sensitized against hegemonic ambitions through developments and experiences of other societies. The Burji, for example, know of poqallas' frequent attempts to acquire political power in neighboring Konso, and that among the Dullay, lineage elders have risen to priestly chiefs. All are aware of the evolution of the dhaama from Dirashe into a centralized political and religious authority. Finally, the polycephalic ethnic groups of southern Ethiopia experienced coercive power in a drastic form in the hierarchical societies with authoritarian command structures peopled by the dominant Amhara and Tigre, to whom they were forced to bow down.

Hegemonic Ambitions among Elected Dignitaries

As a rule, unpopular officials could and can be stripped of their positions, even when these are "hereditary," and their positions themselves may be abolished. Exemplary in this regard are actions taken against the dual office in Burji of the elected woma and dayna, which grew to be a threat for the polycephalic society's order.

A first opportunity for the society to intervene against the woma and dayna arose shortly after the dignitaries' election: they could hinder their induction just prior to their inauguration. Ritual demanded that the two candidates hand over bamboo staffs during a procession to demonstrate their own and their group's agreement with the choice of adversary. At this critical moment in the initiation, members of the community who disagreed with the choice of their designated candidate could take the canes for themselves, thereby suspending the inauguration.

After the woma and dayna were appointed to their positions, the Gada system placed a brake on their ambitions of converting their political power into hegemony. Less rooted than the ganni in the spiritual realm, they were easier to discipline, and moreover had to answer to the community for their behavior. They could not issue arbitrary orders but instead had to work with the councils over which they presided, as primus inter pares and nothing more. Woma and dayna were moreover subordinate to the jurisdiction of the great council, which they were members of, but had to leave when they were under investigation.

In difficult crises, however, not even the multiple provisions for maintaining the balance of power sufficed, as events in Burji at the end of the nineteenth century show. Faced with looming conquest by troops from the hierarchical societies of northern Ethiopia, the woma Guyyo managed to convince a large number of people of the advantages of a strict hierarchical order, and they and his allies worked to dissolve the Gada system until, by 1897, it no longer existed, save for a few residual traces.[31] Guyyo was the first woma to rise to army commander—a post previously held by the hayyu, elected leaders in the Gada system.

In the 1920s, the ganni Ha'pee attained the post of woma as well and became the first balabat of Burji. As such, he collaborated with the conquerors and even participated in the slave trade. His lineage did not elude the population's wrath; his successors were refused the title of ganni.[32]

Though the incumbent woma (southern Burji) and dayna (northern Burji) were bitter antagonists, as holders of the highest leadership positions that the imperial authorities permitted to subordinate ethnic groups, they were pulling in the same direction: those elected after the Italians' withdrawal unceremoniously abolished the vote and were only removed from power by revolutionary cadres in 1974. And yet they remained subordinate to the jurisdiction of the great council—they were incapable of overriding this regulation—and an additional multitude of lesser officials also worked for a certain balance of power.

If, following Pierre Clastres, one looks on executive power as the criterion for hegemony, then for the woma in southern Burji, this existed in the following way: as balabat he had to carry out the instructions of the state administration expressly or otherwise risked a prison sentence. His authority in clan affairs was limited depending on the extent to which elders and other officials acted on his decisions.

Not even the last-serving woma, D'once Guyyo, could rise to the position of despot, despite the backing of the imperial powers.[33]

For the woma, executive power was limited, though ambitious officeholders could expand it in moments of crisis when the society's balance of power was knocked out of equilibrium. Remarkably, there has recently been a fervent debate in Burji for some time as to whether the antagonistic positions of woma and dayna should be restored and instituted alongside elected dignitaries for a certain period. There is great concern about the positions' potential for executive power of a kind abused in the past by various officeholders. The morality tale of a power-hungry woma from the Goona clan serves as a warning here. He issued impracticable orders under threat of violence until the population drove him out of Burji. At a supralocal political meeting in August 2000, speakers drew on his story to buttress their grounds for refusing the rehabilitation of the position of woma. "Tradition ... can thus be understood as a myth that 'establishes normative claims and possesses formative strength.'"[34]

Big Men and Wealth

Even in polycephalic societies, differences in wealth exist. What matters is how far wealth affects social relations; for them, it does not promote dependency, as is common in other societies, especially through possession and control of the means of production. This is evident even in day-to-day behaviors. An affluent "landowner" is expected to be modest and must treat the poor with respect. One way that he does so is to take part in work groups like all others.

It is also seen as unethical to allow others to work for one's benefit without assisting vigorously, if one is healthy enough to do so. This aversion to the exploitation of man by man has clear historic roots in the habitus, as the polycephalic ethnic groups of southern Ethiopia neither possessed slaves nor participated in the slave trade.[35] Still, they were and are aware of the temptation to use wealth to acquire influence, and have complex strategies for confronting it. In essence, these are legal provisions limiting the accumulation of land and goods.

But what do property and ownership signify here? Movable goods and farms can be fairly easily classified as wealth in the Western sense. British social anthropologists describe field land, the most important good in southern Ethiopia, as private property, yet other anthropologists are more cautious here.[36] Officially, the Ethiopian state has owned all land since the conquest of southern Ethiopia. With some regional discrepancies, however, it is not the state but rather the clan or lineage that is looked on as the owner of cultivated field land. Sporadically used plots or pasturage are most often under the authority of regional associations. A farmer can claim exclusive use rights to certain tracts of land, can bequeath them, and can sell or purchase them after consultation with his lineage or territorial unit. Women acquire land through allocations from their husbands and are allowed to manage their income from the harvest (see also the excurses below about ownership conditions).

Concerning the accession of Big Men, it is significant that the accumulation of land is impossible, and land is useless unless a sufficient labor force is available to cultivate it. With the exception of some reguli sacri, prosperity in the rural economy is the reserve of families with numerous able-bodied members. At most, a measure of wealth may accrue through the accumulation of cattle, and in societies that specialize in cattle farming, the number of cattle owned is a sign of affluence. To prevent partly heritable wealth difference from solidifying into stratified layers or classes, the Borana, whose ethics reject both structural inequality and the exploitation of personal advantages, enforce strict rules concerning water use; for instance, no one may possess exclusive rights to a well. Yet a person who digs a well earns social prestige comparable to that resulting from assisting persons in need.[37] Generosity is also incumbent on those who have become wealthy in the growing urban areas.[38] Miserliness, on the other hand, is viewed as contemptible and unbecoming, and can occasion a loss of authority; at assemblies, misers receive scant attention.[39]

Exterior Threats

Exterior threats to polycephalic social forms first arose with the heritable regulus sacer and those dignitaries whose temporary elected appointments evolved into permanent positions. Today it comes from native governmental agencies representing the interests of the state, with *educated people* promoting their own notions of how the societies they stem from should be modernized. In the most favorable cases, state and local interests flow together, and are negotiated politically. This is the case in the Konso town of Buso, where dignitaries were elected to the statist *parlema* and old structures adapted to new demands.[40]

The "egalitarian" guild of craftspeople and traders (fuld'o) have also adapted to the demand for closer ties with the state. Their office in the administrative capital of Konso-Karati is filled with members whom the state authorities designate official representatives, even if, within the union, they hold no particular position of prominence. Urbanization is not a problem for them, as their members may work all over and can maintain annexes elsewhere. Their common interests are represented in supraregional assemblies.

For other polycephalic groups in southern Ethiopia, urbanization, the growth of the diaspora, and since 2010, labor migration to the mines have all proven highly problematic. The radical changes in social forms and conceptions of law that they have occasioned have yet to be researched in a comparative way.[41] The changes wrought by migration and urbanization present challenges not only to polycephalic societies in East Africa but also across the globe and require manifold reactions commensurate with the pertinent historical, political, demographic, and geographic factors. This does not mean that those affected must assimilate completely to their new environment, dissolve their social bonds, or give up their traditional values. Transformation in accordance with the demands of modernity and globalization can also give rise to socially stabilizing forces that may result in new ethnicities based in the urban environment, and elicit a sharpening of individuals' awareness of their identity, as numerous cultural revitalization movements attest.

III.3.   LAW AS CORNERSTONE OF POLYCEPHALIC SOCIAL ORDERS

Polycephalic societies meet their challenges in a variety of ways. For a more precise analysis of how and why they manage to hold themselves together, it is useful to examine the regulations and measures that support and promote their egalitarian social forms as well as the significance of power arrangements within them.

As Clastres has stressed in relation to anarchic societies, power is an immanent necessity of social life, and in the polycephalic societies of southern Ethiopia, people strive for both power, as Hannah Arendt defines it, and certain power relations, the progressive character of which Michel Foucault emphasizes—the power of knowledge, for example. Thus men are expected to acquire socially relevant knowledge in the course of their lives and strive for wisdom, which brings authority, in order to employ both positively, for the common good, in councils and tribunals.

In polycephalic societies, power emerges from the competencies of peers equal in rights who frame their interests in discourses relating to guidelines and rules and to the structure of communal life. Communicative action produces, addresses, and keeps alive the society's central concerns of peace and inner harmony. Internal peace, which is not the same as pacification by a centralized power, forms the basis of cooperation among persons and social institutions. As such, community power works against the hierarchization of society, against stratifications that could give rise to the hegemony of one person over the other.

The apportionment of power among the many generates equilibrium, which in turn actuates competencies in the use of power that themselves depend on social participation. In the tension among partly antagonistic institutions, the individual is constantly faced with political, social, economic, and religious decisions. And participation in decisions that affect society, in part or as a whole, becomes a matter of course.

The law in polycephalic societies is not an isolated domain. Comportment, norms, etiquette, morality, ethos, politics, religion, and law are closely linked in the value system; everyone knows the law, so judges are unnecessary, though this does not prevent an assembly from giving particular regard to a person of great knowledge.[42] Even then, however, judicial power is not entrusted to individuals.

These societies diverge from our own, where law and jurisprudence represent a circumscribed social sphere that regulates conduct without advancing morals or virtues. Law in polycephalic societies is part of lived reality, the worldview, and the cultural heritage. It corresponds neither to an abstraction nor a catalog of applications; rather, it is embodied in the way the community applies and does not apply it. Not every norm violation, not even some we would view as grave, merits judicial treatment. Instead, public ridicule is a popular recourse for norm violations, as many mocking songs embodying well-meaning admonitions attest.

As in all parts of the world, in polycephalic societies the law is sociopolitically mediated and constantly conditioned by history. It is therefore unsurprising that the societies examined here legally regulate domains that for us would fall outside the purview of the law, while others are so manifestly embedded in their habitus that no special legal provisions are required.

A vivid illustration of their legal conceptions is a story told to me by an older man named Aceke in the Dullay region:

> This was a long time ago. My father's brother was not yet a *helho*. It was before his *pulate* feast [which marks the initiation into the Gada system]. He had a girl [as a girlfriend]. Every person who's no longer a child knows the *tampe* [traditional rule, law]: marriage can and should follow immediately on entry into the Gada system; children may not be born before then. This is a law God passed down to our ancestors with the Gada system in the sacred *moore*. The girlfriend of my father's brother got pregnant. Either she didn't want to abort or it didn't work; either way everyone found out. The representatives of the eldest Gada stage came together and resolved to expel the father—in accordance with tradition. He and his girl went into the wilderness [*pata*: a region outside human culture]. He was a strong, clever young man and killed lots of hares and gazelles. The girl bore a healthy son. When it was

time for his generation group's *pulate* feast, the elders allowed him to take part. After his initiation as *helho*, he begged pardon for his behavior and pleaded for another assembly to discuss the reincorporation of his young family. It was agreed that he was an upright person in spite of his grave misdeed. At night, the couple returned from the wilderness and was led blindfolded to the *moore* cult place, where they were covered like two corpses under a winding cloth. During a ceremony the next day, the cloth was removed in the presence of the entire population. They were now fully recognized persons.

Aceke's uncle disobeyed a fundamental rule of the Gada system by usurping a right (to start a family) that did not yet correspond to him. Marriage is considered an important institution for the maintenance of the society. Violating the Gada order with respect to it is a sin against society and its forebears. Offenses to the latter are dangerous; they could curse the land with many kinds of plague. He was therefore irresponsible, as a plague makes all suffer.

Rules for raising a family exist in all the Gada systems of southern Ethiopia. In Konso, Aylota, situated in the east of the heartland, is a settlement for all those who have offended against these rules. Under the pretext of reducing abortions, the "socialist" Derg leadership prohibited the Gada system, although it remained in force in large parts of Ethiopia. Pressure from Western churches opposed to abortion resulted in the annulment of the regulation on marriages and initiation. According to the account of my friend

Shako Otto from Konso, after long meetings, the community amended the Gada system at the end of the 1930s to abolish this rule. A consequence is that Konso has experienced a population explosion of a type unknown before now.[43]

This above example points first to the individual's responsibility to the community, which comprises the living, ancestors, and future generations, and second to what society can and cannot abide. Beside these two important basic principles, further substantial aspects of the legal concept peculiar to this and many other indigenous societies must be taken into account. While there exist unambiguously binding rules—some codified, as in the above case—there are others whose determinants apply more broadly. Hence what we can assess is a kind of "case law" that draws on earlier precedents, is flexible, and adapts to the circumstances at hand. In all instances, this "law" extends beyond mere tradition:

- Law is a domain of social control. In the above, negotiations by a Gada committee concern a breach of norms.
- Committees—not judges—can apply sanctions. In the above, that means expulsion. Not every breach of norms necessitates sanctions.
- The law serves for the collective avoidance of harm. In the above, that entails the blurring of the family order and avoidance of calamities such as plagues.
- The law is an expression of normative value of rituals and myths. In the above, this involves the ritual

conveyance of the couple to the mythical place of origin where the social order was conferred and the ritual purification of their offense as a precondition for resocialization. With their social status fully restored, the couple will, in the future, form part of the decision-making body.

There exists no coercive apparatus for the safeguarding and execution of legal decisions, because one aim of the society is for the meaning, purpose, and validity of the law to be recognized and cherished as a value. Consciousness of law is the fruit of social practice and active participation in communal life, and leaves its mark on the habitus of individuals, who are members and exemplars of the legal community.

The normative sphere shows itself in concepts that inevitably refer back to the cultural heritage as well as the norms and value conceptions anchored therein. This becomes a reference point for reprimands of a given behavior or recommendations for another's comportment. It is significant in this connection that in the above example, the cosmic and earthly orders are interwoven, and within that nexus, as Friedrich Klausberger writes concerning the Gofa, who reside to the northwest of the Burji-Konso Cluster, "the sustaining collective values of the community, such as fertility ... social peace ... justice, and the ordering and legal principles that flow from them ... [rise] to a numinous plane" that grants them legitimacy.[44]

III.3.1. Legal Cases: Brief Introductory Overview

Initial differences from the evaluation of legal cases and offenses in authoritarian states come to light in a selection of legal cases. After discussion with my dialogue partners in polycephalic farming societies, I have listed them here according to significance. Even if the present exposition ignores the flexibility of application, it still offers an initial, albeit rough, frame of reference. The gravest actions are those that appear to threaten the existence of the society and its basic order. There, pertinent rules are often codified, and offenses are examined in assemblies that extend beyond the clan or local group. On the opposite end lies the resolution of conflicts between individuals or small face-to-face groups, the purview of which may be fluid. Indeed, the question of whether a legal matter concerns only a limited circle of individuals or the community at large is a frequent object of discussion.

In the region explored in the present work, the most serious matters are the strict rules for exogamy, which are unambiguously codified. These guarantee the group's physical continuity, social and political reciprocity, and equilibrium among individual ancestral lines. Similarly binding is the ordering of persons by their respective age or generation groups, indicative of specific social functions. The misuse of power and dereliction of duty among dignitaries are also considered grave; these people are obliged to act as exemplars, and their offenses are punished more harshly than those of ordinary people.

Neglect of reciprocal relations, particularly of assistance, as well as absence from community work, memorial services, and assemblies are likewise punishable, and are considered detrimental to the society as a whole. Among agricultural groups in particular, adultery is an offense against human and cosmic order. Insubordination on sacred grounds and offenses against dignitaries are seen as contrary to the community's interests. Homicide, murder, severe bodily injury, and abuse follow the above in terms of gravity. As these offenses do disturb social harmony, they are largely the concern of two opposed parties. Negotiation, rather than strict regulation, is the appropriate procedure for such cases and those that follow. Finally, in order of descending importance, we have arson, theft, fraud, land disputes, nonpayment of debts, disputes over inheritance, and controversies surrounding marriage and divorce. It should be said, though, that in closed settlements, arson is a major offense. Also, before the rise of the Abyssinian Empire, betrayal of secrets to enemy ethnic groups was a grave crime in the agricultural societies under examination.

Marriage rules are also strictly regulated among the pastoralist Borana, as are protocols on the use of natural resources, especially wells. Concerning the last, one can speak of a veritable system of water rights. There are prescribed punishments for offenses against rules demanding mutual aid among clan members, participation in ceremonies, and ownership rights for horses. Punishment for other offenses is generally a matter of negotiation.[45]

Among the Arsi, who practice agriculture and animal husbandry in their settlement area south of Addis Ababa, the law—unusually for a polycephalic society—is codified to a high degree. It is divided into four groups (*woyu*) and recited at every important ceremony. Its main concerns are the protection of people, animals, and objects esteemed according to their ritual significance.[46]

The ordering of offenses by gravity has merely heuristic value and is not at all unproblematic. But it does paint a picture of what requires legal intervention in polycephalic societies. At this point, the cases may appear essentialist, but they cannot be separated from their overarching sociocultural context, against which they must be perceived and evaluated. Here, matters are only objectified into cases in the context of communication.

In the end, what Klausberger writes about the adjudication of offenses among the Gofa is true, cum grano salis, for the populations presented here: "New disputes that lack a precedent to guide their resolution must be examined by those who uphold the law in the context of a scale of values and of culture-bound rules governing sociability. In the individual case, the starting point and measuring rod for decision making is ... how a Gofa man, accustomed to acting moderately and intelligently in accordance with the moral concepts of the community, would comport himself in such a situation."[47] These words make clear the proximity of ethics and law.

III.3.2. Finding Justice

In order to translate aspects of social practice into juristic norms in accord with a society's values, there must be corresponding behaviors that lend them legitimacy. The legal legitimation and acceptance of social norms implies a number of procedures for infractions of problematic cases:

- Extensive *negotiation through community discussion*, for which different assemblies are stipulated. Ad hoc groups are also organized to look at specific cases. Generally this occurs during personal disputes between members of different clans or regional groups. If they reach an agreement or are ordered to do so by those around them, they seek out one or several neutral mediators. In urban environments, where traditional structures retain a hold on consciousness, but are only weakly present, this procedure plays an important role in ensuring social stability.[48]

- *Spontaneous, generally aggressive judgments* of witnesses against those caught *in flagranti*. Spontaneous judgments against persons caught in the act of committing a misdeed are considered legitimate. Hence a person being robbed may beat the thief if they catch them in the act. Nowadays, it is unlikely that a murderer will be killed, but they are still wise to seek refuge immediately.

- *Secret accords in meetings*, especially for offenses in the numinous or religious sphere. Secret meetings generally concern religious dignitaries whose behavior the populace no longer accepts. The meetings are secret to protect their members from the supernatural powers of the reguli sacri, who can employ his spiritual powers to do harm. There is little information about these proceedings or their participants.[49]

- *Interethnic meetings*, when aggrieved parties belong to different population groups. Generally, before a hearing on such legal cases begins, representatives of the respective population groups will meet to discuss procedure. After bellicose conflicts, it is often postmenopausal women from enemy ethnic groups who establish first contact and prepare the ground for further negotiations. (Traditionally women are not killed in war.)

The examination of legal questions by committee is an essential recourse for the production and preservation of cohesion in these societies. This is evident from the following case, which was scrutinized by an elected committee of some twenty men of various ages in Konso. I was invited to witness the entire discussion, which took around five hours. The proceedings and conduct evinced are representative of those in many similar situations.

Two men, around twenty-three years old, both from the same place, had quarreled. Rather than settling their dispute at home, they later made a show of their ill will elsewhere, and then did the same after walking to the home of a dignitary and finding him away. The first item before the assembly was not the root of their disagreement but instead the fact of the quarrel itself, especially at a place as symbolically significant as the home of a dignitary, where assemblies also took place.

An elder opened the meeting, and exhorted the participants to speak with discipline and calm: "Whoever wishes to speak may do so, uttering anything he pleases, as long as he raises his hand and waits his turn. Speak freely and politely; when uttering a condemnation, you should not shout or speak loudly, but rather with a quiet tone, slowly, politely, and patiently. And always speak the truth. That is the right path for a discussion." To begin, one member briefly outlined the case in a neutral and matter-of-fact tone. A second and then third repeated what he had said in the form of questions, something like: Was it not so? Did these young men inform the elders? No, they were silent.

Commentary followed. The first speaker drew a comparison: "When a mother readies a meal, she makes portions for the father, for the older and the younger children. The portions have a name, and all must wait until they get something from the mother. Our two children (here, the quarrelers) must learn that there are rules, and we must stay here today until all of us have had our turn to speak and until we find a solution for the case." The second speaker told the story of the blind man who was invited to a ceremonial slaughter.

The people gave him pieces of meat, but he refused them all. Even the best two pieces he groused about. Finally someone stood up and brought him kidneys, and the blind man was radiant; that was what he had wanted. The people upbraided him. Why did you complain and get us into a tizzy? Why didn't you just say what you wanted? Right, and so why didn't these two young men come to us and explain their problem instead of feuding about it? Why must they make difficulties for us? Now we all have to come together and leave our work behind. They deserve a harsh punishment that will teach them a lesson. None of us should go home until then.

Only now did the dignitary in whose house the two had quarreled take the floor:

What kind of home is my house for me now? You have to stamp out the embers before they turn into fire. If you don't put them out right away, they will destroy the town. Children play behind their father's back, and when they go too far, he gives them a spanking. When these two started quarreling, we fined them six *birr*. But they didn't learn. They came to my house, they broke my chair, they beat my representative, they beat my wife, they beat me in my absence.

Then, turning to the offenders, he asked,

Do you know of the punishment of our elders, those who founded our culture, which I cannot fail to mention? Do you even know what *kaara* is? That's thirty oxen. And do you know what *haramatta* means? Those are the hairs on your head—uncountable, in other words. I will not speak to you about the roots of your quarrel until you have reconciled and paid the price for your behavior.

To my astonished question of what had actually happened in the house, my neighbor replied, "The young men didn't beat his wife. But their quarrel was *like* a slap in the face."

Another speaker told the following story:

A man went to a house at night. When he felt a pressure in his bowels, he squatted on the road to answer nature's call. No one saw him do it. Soon, another man came behind him. He stepped in the excrement, but didn't see what it was. So he felt it with his hand. Still, he couldn't quite say what it was. Then he sniffed, and he dirtied his nose. These boys here didn't even tell us of their quarrel, and they still haven't asked for forgiveness. In this way, they've dirtied our entire society, from the simplest helper to our elected speaker.

The next turned to the two young men, was more conciliatory, and addressed them again as children: "Now you are very young, strong, and rich, but don't think you can live alone and without help." He gave as an example a proverb about bees and compared it with their own society.

The debate went on another two hours or so. Without playing down the two men's conduct, those in attendance tried to mollify the aggrieved party and soften the punishment. In the end, it was moderate, and the verdict was unanimous. Extreme discipline characterized the proceedings. None talked among themselves, and there were no interruptions, no offensive gestures, at most occasional nodding or interjections signaling agreement. All who raised their hands to speak had the opportunity to do so, including the wrongdoers (one of whom gave a fifteen-minute speech) and their advocates. Even the speech of a man who might be termed a "vagrant" enjoyed undivided attention.[50] When all present had offered their points of view and no one else wished to speak, the young men asked forgiveness of all present, acknowledged their misconduct publicly, and placed their fine in a wooden box. The elders there blessed them both and sanctioned the restoration of social unity. A bowl of roasted corn was passed around, and everyone ate from it, including the two men who had stood trial. Only then was the cause of their quarrel discussed.[51] Each man present received a small portion of the fine that the young men had paid at the meeting's end, and they spent it on restorative millet beer in the company of the young men, who were no longer looked on as criminals.[52]

We still lack the key for interpretation here, but many questions arise that should be debated going forward: What is the role of the two men in this society? Why was their quarrel so significant that a supraregional assembly was summoned? Is the cause of the quarrel irrelevant? What rules and norms were violated? What is the role of the scene of the offense, and to what extent were third parties affected? What is the dignitary's significance? How should references to his injuries be understood? What is the composition of the assembly, and who takes part in discussion? Are there hierarchies? The accused can clearly defend themselves. Do they have legal assistance in doing so? Does the discussion evince a formal structure? How do assembly members proceed, what arguments do they offer, and how? How does the verdict come about? Is it relevant for the society at large? What is the purpose of the proceeding? Is punishment key, or do other factors, like edification or understanding, play a role? Do the accused recognize the verdict? What is the significance of their apology? Is it penitence or subordination? What is the meaning of the ritual at the end of the proceedings? Can the accused file an appeal?

III.3.3. Assemblies and Councils

From small work groups to supraregional meetings, only slight formal and functional differences characterize different gatherings and assemblies, irrespective of their complexity. In principle, all grown persons are considered equal, and customarily, organization and moderating functions fall to one of the elders. This speaker or moderator is a primus inter pares lacking in executive power. Depending on the assembly's size, he has representatives and assistants alongside him as well as people who summon the assembly and announce the verdict. Jurisdiction rests with the assembly alone, not with an individual or legal elite.

Gatherings of hereditary groups (whether families, lineages, moieties, or clans) should be looked on as legal institutions. The eldest in a hereditary group is frequently the moderator and organizer. For nonfamily-related deliberations, the assembly always elects the moderator along with their representatives and assistants for a limited period of time, or designates their functions. All adults can take part, and will be expected to, if the matter at hand concerns them. This is true for women too, though in large assemblies extending beyond kinship groups, men predominate by far. Extensive, supraregional assemblies are made up of chosen representatives of subgroups.

Gatherings take place in established settings, often at ceremonial sites. They are generally called as needed, and the dates usually set with reference to the calendar of feast days. Discussions touch on everyday problems as well as economic, political, and juristic matters, and the composition of participants frequently remains the same despite the multiplicity of themes. Legal assemblies are announced as such, and for the accused and certain dignitaries, attendance is mandatory.

The mediation of conflicts by individuals or small groups can be looked on as a purely legal procedure. But when a legal matter touches on the public interest, as often occurs in polycephalic societies, the quarrel becomes political, and the competencies of legal and political assemblies may bleed together until they become indistinguishable. I will begin by examining the formal framework and function of assemblies of certain ethnic groups in more detail.

Burji   Among the Burji, every city quarter or district (*geere*) consists of various neighborhoods (*olla*). Small disputes are resolved at the gathering place of an olla; clan and geere courts address legal cases in which the aggrieved parties live in the same geere or belong to the same clan. The matters that come before them are similar—inheritance and land use disputes, personal injury, and debts—and occasionally the two institutions merge. The elected "head" of the geere organizes and moderates the geere courts, and an elected dignitary whose term is for life does the same for clan courts. For assemblies to be quorate, all persons and groups affected by the matter under discussion must take part. Interclan courts come together when disputants belong to different clans. These cases usually deal with bride prices, divorce, and personal injury and murder.

Large, supraregional councils overriding the geere and clan examine cases that these groups are unfit to regulate, such as because they affect the entire region or Burji population as a whole. Large assemblies (*hidittinka oolcoo* or *gorsooma*), which involve both northern and southern Burji, nowadays take place in the administrative capital, Soyama, with around a hundred representatives. Outside Burji town (Boohee Burji) is a place reserved for oath ceremonies, once the ultima ratio for quarrels irresolvable through legal means alone.

Dullay   Among Dullay speakers, every ethnic group possesses a council of elders (*ħaad'ike 'akkad'a*) as the highest assembly. At one time, all the men of the highest Gada rank belonged to it, but as the influence of the Gada system waned in the imperial period, the council came to consist only of select married men. Holdovers from the Gada system are the posts of hayyo and *pitte*, which the council of elders chooses for each subregion for a specific period of time. Their duties include making useful recommendations at assemblies, organizing incidental work, overseeing violations of the law, rooting out troublemakers in the case of feuds, and understanding legal concepts, in which the pitte is more experienced and knowledgeable than the elders. Every person may turn to the pitte in his region to request that he submit a claim to the regional council, as in the case of theft. Supraregional councils of elders from all groups debate norms, problems, political and ceremonial measures, and communal labor in agriculture; they also decide on military actions and peace agreements. They provide a forum for serious infringements that might bring crop failures or other misfortunes to the territory. The council of elders sets the sowing period and other important dates, and takes measures against animal diseases and similar threats.[53] The competencies and status of the council assembly are evident in an episode from the 1970s, during the imperial era, that affected me personally: a visit to the burial forest (*elme*) and grave of the poqolho Rasko in Gollango. I had discussed burial rituals and the arrangement of the hereditary grave of the poqolho with a number of older men, among them the hayyo, the deceased's brother, and his son, Sailo Rasko (serving poqolho and balabat). They all requested that I document the gravesite, and for that purpose a seer (*so'akko*) was put at my disposal. A few days after my visit to the burial forest, the seer was called to an ad hoc gathering. Members of the council accused him of arbitrary behavior and stressed that consultation with the council was required before any visit to the burial forest. To my objection that the poqolho had granted the seer permission to visit his father's grave, they explained that he had no right to do so, and that the seer should have known that a spiritually significant place of that kind could only be visited in rare circumstances with the consultation and blessing of the community. I was excluded from later assemblies and never found out how the affair was settled. Probably the seer asked for forgiveness, for he assured me that no harm came to him, and he continued to be held in high esteem. What matters here is that only the assembly was competent to evaluate the nature of this affair with regard to religious norms and whether their violation might have effects on the entire community.

The elected assemblies vanished with the revolution, and political power devolved to the farmers' associations (*kebele*) that the Derg had established. The regime of the time demanded a parliament composed of political parties. Regardless, informal networks of elders remained politically active for decades. Since 2000 in Gollango, there has been an assembly (*maapara*) of elders and traditional dignitaries working for the development of their region. When I visited in 2003, the maapara had achieved authentic consensus in the most important decisions, and also determined whether and when legal proceedings should take place. This approach clearly remains successful, as little use is made of state courts.

Konso In Konso, the large assemblies were confined to the towns (*paleta*). If disputes arose among them, supraregional poqalla, who lived outside the settlement, were generally brought in, but as arbitrators and not as judges. Before the imperial regime introduced the post of balabat, elders' councils exclusively administrated the sovereign cities. The most significant were the councils from individual parts of the cities (*kanta*). Even today they handle matters of public interest and legal cases, although they are obliged to comply with the state's guidelines.[54] Assemblies are organized by the *aapa timpaa*, the keeper of the holy drum, symbol of peaceful conviviality as well as law and order.[55] He structures debate, at least in part, but as primus inter pares, not as judge.[56] There are also periodic "extraordinary" gatherings, if the elders deem them necessary, to emphasize common moral and legal values, and warn against misconduct.

During the Derg mandate, the Konso kebele were official political assemblies, but traditional gatherings took place alongside them. After the overthrow of the Derg, the kebele declined in importance, yet they continue to control the lower jurisdiction, which may impose sentences of up to three months. Traditional assemblies exercise de facto control over Konso villages and hence legal pluralism exists here.[57] The present-day regime demands that locally elected parliaments (*parlamma*) administrate the cities, and elections typically occur in consultation with traditional assemblies. Elizabeth Watson is right to see this as a marked change in the relationship between traditional authority and the state, for elders have recuperated their rank and even play key roles in the state administration. Their membership in parliament gives them new authority, and their new posts bind them to their earlier responsibilities.[58] The councils of the ethnic groups of the Gamo Highlands possess similar structures and functions, and there too, historical changes have had the same impact.[59]

Borana   The Borana have a complex system of assemblies, but for our purposes, a discussion of their basic principles suffices.[60] These immediate neighbors of the Burji-Konso Cluster have had great success in their gatherings, and continue to do so today, serving as an example for southern Ethiopia and northern Kenya. Here the Borana are representative of other Oromo groups whose social ordering follows a similar democratic orientation.[61]

At the local level, the settlement (*cora olla*) and clan (*cora gosa*) assemblies form the basic political and juridical units. They discuss everyday matters, regulate access rights to resources and marriage transactions, and give consultations concerning aid to members in need.[62] In principle, only fathers of families are full members in assemblies, as they alone possess herds and are capable of paying any requisite fines. Older members have great influence, and their advice is in demand, while younger people may participate in order to learn. Supraregional clan gatherings with more than a hundred representatives occur in alternating settings and examine cases that cannot be resolved locally.[63]

The system is made more complex by the inclusion of Gada group assemblies, which maintain peaceful coexistence and cooperation among regional groups and clans.[64] From the fourth grade (*kuusa*) onward, every active Gada class has its own committee, which is further subdivided in turn, and chooses one, or rarely more than one, hayyuu as speaker. In contrast to the ethnic groups mentioned earlier, they acquire judicial knowledge essential for their position in special settlements with ritual status, but may not employ it as judges; instead, they use it to aid in reaching consensus.[65] For Eike Haberland, this "fullest democratic freedom" in Borana legal proceedings is "likely the best warrant of equality before the law."[66] The Borana divide power across different planes and groups from settlements and clans as well as through the Gada system and its cross-generational committees. This apportionment transforms hierarchies into balanced opposition. Taken as a whole, the assorted assembly types and their miscellaneous compositions and competencies have a pyramidal structure. At the summit is the All Borana Assembly (*gummi gayoo*), organized by the reigning Gada representatives; it meets every eight years and has up to three thousand participants. There, representatives of committees and interested Borana exchange their thoughts about national concerns and discuss cases that local assemblies cannot clarify.[67] More important still is their legislative function: only the gummi gaayoo has the power to issue new laws; these are validated in the larger framework of Borana law and are binding within it. Mandates from the state must be covered too. In the autumn 2012 gummi gaayoo, older laws were modified and provisions supporting the education of girls were adopted.[68]

The Borana distinguish between *seera* (formally pronounced laws) and *aadaa* (traditionally proscribed behaviors). Seera comprise compulsory legal principles negotiated in groups. Aadaa mirror traditional norms that arise from ordinances handed down by the ancestors, make reference to the spiritual, and in that relation, are legally binding.[69]

III.3.4. Prioritization of Legal Cases and Their Sociopolitical Significance

This overview has shown that different legal cases possess varying degrees of significance, an assessment of which determines the way that the responsible groups examine these cases. But to what extent does the prioritization of legal cases already preserve a measure of antihegemonic momentum? Does the mere fact of problematizing (or not) a given proceeding in legal terms clarify for the society what is relevant for the avoidance of hegemony? Or are legal decisions in principle an inadequate index for freedom from hegemony, given their general ambivalence along with their aptitude for employment in support of both state violence and "egalitarian" power?

The gravity assigned to a given case is determined by a society's values and therefore may provide a first indication. Let's take as an example the secret violation of field rights, which is prosecutable in both statist and polycephalic societies. If the plaintiff is a state subject, he will look to the power of the state monopoly on violence to protect his rights. In the end, there are similar provisions in polycephalic societies, where committees defend the rights of the plaintiff. This case thus does nothing to elucidate my initial question. But there must be examples of differentiation. For instance, our conception of marriage rules differs notably from that of many non-Western societies. A balanced ratio of reciprocal rights and duties among people and groups is a precondition for the successful functioning of polycephalic societies, and marriage being a privileged domain, it is essential that matrimonies engage partners outside an individual's family line. Claude Lévi-Strauss has convincingly shown that the incest prohibition is a prerequisite for human society, and obedience to it is required for the development of broader social ties. In polycephalic societies, the ubiquitous incest prohibition extends into highly complex exogamy rules.[70] Among the Gumuz (in western Ethiopia and Sudan), a breach of the incest taboo is considered so monstrous that atonement on earth is impossible, and punishment is entrusted to cosmic powers through placing a curse.[71]

A clear difference from monarchies is evident here. While it is true that certain marriage proscriptions apply to the latter, exogamy rules are normally constricted rather than expanded, and serve to consolidate a noble line or dynasty. In sacred monarchies in particular, this may lead to the complete revocation of the incest prohibition and to sibling marriage, as in the Old Kingdom in Egypt.[72]

In many polycephalic societies, the harshest punishments are reserved for the transgression of exogamy laws.[73] Rules are clear, and there is almost no leeway. Infringement is an assault on society's basic principles; among the Dullay, it demands an expiation ceremony for the entire ethnic group, even after the delinquent has been expelled from the territory.

It is therefore unsurprising that marriage bonds are a far from private affair, and constitute a binding contract between family and lineage. Marriage, divorce, and associated inheritance arrangements are integral concerns of the legal system.[74] Before a wedding takes place, there are legally binding negotiations between the families or lineages concerned over the implied economic transactions. These generally stretch on for years. These transactions affect many households, and while this reinforces social bonds, it can also lead to quarrels. Resolution is typically the responsibility of families and the mediators they have employed, but frequently, the committees described above are involved. In some groups, in-laws' bride duty is more important than material transactions.

In mountain farming communities, adultery is a grave offense against the social order, which is seen as a divine legacy.[75] Pastoral cattle farmers view it a bit differently. Among them, adultery in secret may be punished, while for the Borana, extramarital sex is permitted but also subject to certain regulations.[76]

In most instances, adultery is dealt with by affected parties and their relatives. But among mountain farmers, it demands ritual purification to ward off danger to the society. This is especially true if the wife of a religious dignitary is involved. Then, a higher committee must intervene.[77]

Rape, like marriage and divorce, is in principle an affair between affected families or lineages. The kidnapping of brides is countenanced so long as the young woman agrees beforehand—for instance, if she wishes to escape arranged marriage with another partner. The father of the kidnapper will address the woman's father either directly or through an intermediary to bid forgiveness as well as to sanction the marriage between his son and the woman who has given her consent.

Theft Theft is seen not as a conflict between victim and perpetrator but rather as an unsolidaristic act posing a danger to the community. There are serious provisions for its punishment. The degree to which theft may destroy a community is made clear in the Burji myth, which is also familiar to the Konso and Borana: theft of a sacrificial lamb and the conflicts arising from it produced irrevocable divisions among the Burji, Konso, and Borana, who had lived together in peace until then.[78]

The severity of thefts depends on circumstances; the theft of a sacrificial animal is graver than that of a mere lamb, as it affects socioreligious interests. The prior history and character of the thief are considered, as is the material or ideal value of the stolen object. A petty thief, caught for the first time, is normally punished with ridicule. "The sorry character is too weak even to chop down a dry tree"—this and similar commentaries scorn a person who has made off with a bit of firewood. After a second offense, people will observe how the thief behaves in the future. Depending on the nature of the theft, various committees will sit in judgment of the wrongdoer. Thieves must compensate for damages that they have caused, but also receive additional punishment.[79] Under certain circumstances, minor thefts,

which for us would count as the stealing of food for immediate consumption, are permissible. Half orphans, for
example, are given a sack and small knife, and are permitted to purloin slivers of meat from the butchers at the
market.

The Konso punish impenitent thieves harshly. At one
time, notorious thieves in Buso were "flung to their death
from a nearby cliff."[80] This was likely spontaneous justice,
since none of these communities are known to have sanctioned the death penalty. These actions seem to have been
collective on the part of the Gada youths of the time, and
as such, protected the individual participants from retribution by the thieves' relatives: where everyone is guilty, no
one is.

Arson In traditional settlements, cooking is done in
straw-roofed houses over open flames and neighbors help
each other with the hearth. The danger of fire is therefore
high. If one person does something to cause another's
house to catch fire, the territorial assembly must clarify
first whether an accident or arson has occurred. Even in
the absence of motive, there is discussion of compensation. If those involved do not reach agreement, an interclan
committee is summoned to settle the matter. If the plaintiff remains stubborn, perhaps because they suspect bad
intentions behind the fire, the decision passes over to a
supraregional committee.

Wrongdoers must pay damages for premeditated fires.
Additional punishments apply depending on the danger to

others—such as whether the fire was set in a closed settlement or on an isolated farm. A drunk who willfully set his neighbor's farmhouse alight in the densely built Konso city of Buso, and thus risked burning down an entire quarter of the town, received a particularly harsh punishment, being exiled from the territory.[81]

Overstepping Competencies The law's antihegemonic function is evident in the controls placed on dignitaries. Since they must serve as exemplars, their infractions are punished more harshly than those of ordinary persons. In the sacred kingdoms of Ethiopia, as in feudal states in general, the "nobility" enjoyed special privileges. In polycephalic societies, in contrast, the powerful are watched over closely by their fellow men. Abuse of position and overstepping competencies—attempting to broaden their assigned powers—are especially flagrant offenses. The Burji admonish a newly appointed ganni to avoid politics, and concern himself exclusively with peaceful conviviality and religious matters. If these warnings are ineffective, the penalties increase in severity. Dignitaries who neglect their duties may have their position revoked, and they themselves can be tried; their estates are subject to confiscation and redistribution; and in the worst cases, the dignitaries may be expelled from the territory. In Burji, the council required a woma to testify before the people for an alleged infraction.[82] And Bamalle, the successor to the aforementioned pretender to supraregional regulus sacer in Kosno, and who hoped to become "tribal chief over all of Konso" with Italian support in the 1930s, lost his farm to fire.

Naturally, abuse of power is a crime in democratic state societies as well. But there, condemnation falls on the accrual of personal advantage, such as through corruption. One need not think of Silvio Berlusconi to know that this is something political elites have long accepted with a greater or lesser degree of indifference. Meanwhile, state law says nothing about the expansion of dominance and competencies, perhaps relying on the currently accepted constitution and corresponding political regulations. The jurist Carl Schmitt vindicated the broadening of powers with his famous formulation that "the sovereign decides the state of exception." It is noteworthy that at the Nuremberg trials, the transformation of democracy into dictatorship did not appear on the list of indictments against the National Socialists. Indeed, a liberal interpretation could affirm that the Nazis' assumption of power did not run contrary to the law until after Paul von Hindenburg's death. The indictments cited neither the Nazi takeover nor the revocation of parliamentary control over the state monopoly on power, but instead the later violation of modern European legal norms.[83]

If certain dignitaries in polycephalic societies managed to expand their dominance, the fault lay not in the existing legal framework but rather in external historical contingencies, such as threats or invasions coming from imperial Abyssinia. These are the very cases that sensitized the population to focus on potential concentrations of power and thematize them in public discussions. Hence, native persons who held high positions in the state apparatus could at times face prosecution by indigenous courts. Among the Borana, such an officeholder received the worst possible punishment for exercising his influence in a field reserved for traditional authorities.[84] Typical here is an incident from among the Burji in the southern Ethiopian administrative capital of Awasa: the leader of the state authorities, himself a Burji, arrested an elected traditional representative of a town ward for administering donations with the allegation that this action fell under purview of the state. The *oolcoo-ana* invoked his constitutionally guaranteed right to act in accordance with traditional rules. When the state official publicly boxed his ears, the oolcoo-ana placed a curse on him. Three days later, the man fell gravely ill and freed the oolcoo-ana, who had been arrested in the interim. This instance of usurpation of authority by the state administration shocked the Burji in their homeland and the diaspora all the way to Nairobi.[85]

Even those without special functions must be wary of the dereliction of duty; there are punishments for misconduct in situations important for group solidarity, from neglecting assistance to failure to attend work group assignments, gatherings, or funerals. Though inconsequential today, refusal of hearth fire still remains an effective punishment. Symbolically, it represents a temporary exclusion from society. In polycephalic societies, neglect of solidaristic obligations incurs not physical violence but instead a loosening or rupture of reciprocal relations.

Those who insistently evade their duties and fail to heed admonitions can expect further social exclusion. Personal contact with such people and their families is avoided, and no one assists them with their fieldwork or when they are ill. Until they offer a public apology, they may not attend feasts and rituals, and no one will take their side in legal proceedings. Banishment is the highest form of isolation assignable as well as the most serious punishment.[86]

In societies with a functioning Gada system, the existence of the polycephalic order itself ensures obedience to rules. Great value is attached to respect for it. Those who violate the orders of generation or age groups along with the social roles that they imply can reckon on harsh retribution. To my knowledge, there is no room for negotiation; this is a decree not subject to debate.

Antihegemonic components are visible even in the traditional status of murder. While present-day southern Ethiopians approve of the prosecution of murder by state authorities, a long prison term or death sentence for a murderer is of little use to the victim's relatives. Traditional law provides for the loss of work capacity or a breadwinner, and traditional assemblies continue to rule over such matters. Compensation was long seen as more significant than a corpse hung from a tree in revenge, and the institution of blood vengeance did not exist. Even if enraged relatives or friends of a victim could kill a fleeing murderer with impunity, the importance of asylum was still emphasized, as it offered the chance for negotiation and kept lynch law at bay. This is why murder suspects could no longer be pursued once they had reached a socially recognized, permanently accessible legal refuge. Even today, fugitives rely on the protection of such sanctuaries, in the main ceremonial grounds or the farms of reguli sacri. In southern Ethiopia, as in many other regions, sanctuary status is inseparably bound to sacred functions—or as Bertram Turner expresses it, the idea of protection in space is a materialization of a numinous plane of the religious made manifest in refuges for those in search of safety.[87] The roots of this idea reach far back in the past; its main expression today is the asylum offered by the church.[88] In Christian Ethiopia, the protective function of church asylum had and continues to have significant social, political, and legal weight; the largest sanctuary territory lies in the radius of the churches of Axum.[89] In southern Ethiopia, holy grounds are closely related to ancestors and the divine, and thus to a higher order that superintends the human one. As extrajudicial spaces, they offer protection to fugitives within the "sphere of influence of the holy."[90] Disregard of asylum rights is not only a violation of the law but also constitutes blasphemy.[91]

While not a specific feature of anarchic society, these spaces do furnish protection from the state monopoly on violence. The right to grant asylum, for the sacred king and regulus sacer, is an augmentation of authority, but as spiritual figures they are obliged to the numinous and, being themselves the highest magistrates, may not touch fugitives who have been granted asylum. Like the chief described by Clastres, they are restrained by the power they possess. Particularly when sacred persons lack judicial functions, the right to protection, in polycephalic societies, can sustain anarchic formations, being itself an element of anarchy: a realm in which no person has power over another.

The institution of asylum makes possible the resolution of conflicts, providing the prerequisites for negotiation by ensuring adequate time for debate. It opens a protective space outside society until a peaceable and satisfactory solution is reached. In the case of murder, only after the perpetrator has passed some time in asylum and tempers have calmed do negotiations between his relatives and those of the victim begin, through a mediator or mediating assembly at an interlineage meeting. A murder case being, in essence, a dispute between two parties, unless there is doubt as to the wrongdoer, there is not always a supraregional council or Gada assembly. The affected parties must always reach an agreement; otherwise, those who have refused the mediators' efforts at conciliation are ostracized or even, in extreme cases, exiled from the territory.[92] Following the successful resolution of negotiations, the murderer is reintegrated into society with a reconciliation and purification ritual, and may leave his sanctuary afterward; frequently his bloodguilt requires a purification ceremony for the entire region.[93] All this takes place irrespective of whether a state court has convicted the murderer.

The above shows how the society and its law are oriented to harmony and balance, avoiding fractures through, for example, blood vengeance. Recourse to state courts that neglects mediation as implemented in feuds or within families and neighborhoods is also an offense to the community with its harmony-oriented principles; these proceedings minimize damages to the society at large, as complainants do not sing out their grievances for all to hear.

The significance attributed to libel shows the importance of the individual in these societies. When libel proceedings take place, compensation is relatively high.

In contemporary legal pluralism, mediation is a conscious and adequate means of holding state power at bay. But there are other aspects of the law that may facilitate hegemony. An illustration is when offenses against dignitaries weigh more harshly than those against other persons. Still, the punishments prescribed for crimes of this sort are never so drastic in polycephalic societies as in monarchies, where offenses against the ruler may lead to execution.[94] Though capital punishment is theoretically possible for certain crimes in polycephalic societies, the extent of its implementation is an open question, save for cases where it has affected the vital religious sphere. In Burji, people can only recall the killing of a single rain priest. It appears that in assemblies, the death penalty has merely been invoked as a threat in order to symbolically emphasize the gravity of a misdeed.

Excursus: Property Relationships Movable objects are considered personal possessions. This includes tools, work utensils, and men's weapons as well as their jewelry, ceremonial objects, and beehives. Women, on the other hand, possess kitchen utensils, jewelry, clothing, coffee bushes near their home, and the money made from such tasks as beer brewing. Here, the use of our concept of property is justifiable. Men and women make decisions in common about the expenditure of household funds. Among farmers, cattle are property of the family, but animals and smaller livestock (goats and sheep) may be privately exploited by husbands, wives, sons, or daughters. As long as she is married, the house that a woman lives in with her children belongs to her. But another man may only enter it with permission from her husband.

Usage Rights to Field Land At first glance, few restrictions seem to apply to the private use of field land, and some ethnologists have considered it private property. Helmut Straube surmises "that use-intensive fields where much work has been invested are transferable individual property, while extensively cultivated field land, pastures, and the technical constructions required for irrigation are generally held in common."[95] In fact, outlying zones with pastureland and unirrigated fields used with rotating crops are at the disposal of all members of a society, provided all take part in communal clearings and guarding the field against wild animals. Those who make land arable often exercise heritable usage rights.

Restrictions on Landownership Categorical definitions frequently give rise to problematic explanations and equivalencies. In our culture, *private ownership* is a concept anchored in law; the more appropriate concept, to the degree that such exists, would be *private property*. Any exposition of property relations should rely less on imported concepts than on observations concerning the practices of those groups under consideration. Concepts related to property are inevitably inseparable from the societal context. In this light, David Graeber refers to C. B. Macpherson and his concept of possessive individualism, stating that in the West, people view themselves more and more as isolated individuals, and see their relationship to the world as defined by ownership rather than by sociality.[96] This does not hold for polycephalic societies, at least in the present discussion.

In the Burji-Konso Cluster, the household can generally bequeath the fields surrounding the home, or lease them, divvy them up, give them away, or even sell them, but there are always restrictions on these dispositional rights. The consent of several people is necessary, the number of fields sold cannot be arbitrary, and only certain people have the right to purchase. Once, in Očollo, a man was expelled from the territorial assembly because he had sold land to Amhara—in other words, to foreigners.[97] If possible, transfers should be to members of the broader family, and must be discussed with the elders and one's wife.

As a rule, the rights of lineages or clans and territorial groupings should be respected, even where, as landowners, they play only a nominal role. Lineages and clans only rarely possess land close to a settlement. But if a family has no heirs, its land will fall to the lineage, and the lineage will then redistribute it.

Before selling land to others outside the lineage—to pay a fine to state courts, for example—a person will ask them for financial assistance. If they cannot help, he may sell the land with the agreement of them and his neighbors, who have rights of first purchase. Comparable rules are in place for leases, which have come to arise more recently.

A sophisticated system of rules applies within the household. While land "belongs" to the head of household, the use of land, and especially its proceeds, are in the hands of the wives or sons, though large expenditures must be discussed with the father.

Upon marriage, every woman obtains fields reserved for her use from her husband. She loses this entitlement if she is divorced. When a son is old enough to participate in a work group, he receives a small plot of land and may join in discussions concerning how the proceeds are spent. Cattle are family property if purchased by the father or mother. If the son buys them, they belongs to him. Even privately owned animals may only be sold with the permission of other family members.

Seed is property of the family, and all must contribute to its cost. The father determines when sowing takes place, and seed may only be taken in his presence.

Dignitaries as Landowners and State Land   Finally, cultivated field land belongs to the clan or lineage, and the regulus sacer is responsible for it. He may be considered its owner in a spiritual sense, but hardly in an economic one; but again, this is a polarization derived from our own conceptual bases and does not really apply here. Cautiously, I might designate him a "steward" of the land. He is responsible for ratifying land distribution. Under the reinterpretation of traditional law during the imperial period, those appointed balabat used their position to appropriate significant landholdings with the state's support.

Following the socialist revolution and current constitution, all land is state property, and farmers pay a land tax to use it. But this statute, even if applied across the country, barely influences day-to-day practice. If a person cannot pay his debts, he "lends" his creditors a piece of land as a substitute. The state's claim to ownership of all land has had significant consequences, however: native groups have been stripped of large territories to comply with lease agreements with Israel, Saudi Arabia, and India. Here, the state implements its formal law to the detriment of local laws. For now, this process has left the southern Ethiopian hill country in peace, with the exception of the valley floors, because (at least for the present) investors appear uninterested in it.[98]

Relations among Pastorialists (Borana) Traditionally, neither private landownership nor exclusive pasture rights exist, though there are rules for reasonable usage.[99] The clan or lineage has certain access rights even over cattle. In day-to-day life, they belong to married family men, and the heads of the family are responsible for their respective herds.[100] Ownership of "natural resources" lies with patrilineal kinship groups, while use rights for pastureland are regulated among the clans. Wells are dug by members of an extended family or large kin group, and are their heritable possession. The clans, however, have strict rules covering their use.

Cattle-owning families are expected to help community members in distress, such as by lending them milk cows. This is of great importance within the clans. Women depend on their husbands economically, and each man should leave sufficient cows at the disposal of his wives and widowed mother for use. The women alone may use, distribute, or sell their milk. A woman owns her house, which she builds for herself with other women shortly after her wedding, and lives in until her death or departure.

*   *   *

Among the most explicitly defined (codified) legal domains among field and cattle farmers is inheritance law. It cannot be classed among the egalitarian legal provisions, but it is in no way opposed to them either. It differs little from inheritance law in other patrilineal societies and favors the eldest son. Since levirate marriage hardly still exists, men must care for their widowed mothers. Only recently has it been possible for women to become heiresses when no male heir exists. In polycephalic societies, inheritance law assures that younger brothers do not have to hire themselves out. An older brother, for example, may not sell off land if his younger brothers have none of their own. If a land bequeathal is insufficient, disadvantaged parties can turn to their lineage, which may assign them land in the outer districts. If there is tension among younger brothers, the eldest may resolve it so long as the others agree with his doing so. Here, the family is the smallest legal unit. If it cannot reach consensus, the lineage or clan assembly will arbitrate. In rural areas, jurisdiction remains with the local community.

III.4. NEGOTIATION PROCESSES AND OUTCOMES

In polycephalic ethnic groups, the process and outcome of negotiations are similar among settled agricultural societies and mobile cattle ranching ones. Even content-wise, there are numerous parallels, though the different modes of production bring their own specific issues. Among the Borana, for instance, the construction and use of wells is a perennial topic of debate.

Given that the fuld'o negotiation process was examined above, here I will pay particular attention to proceedings in the committees of the Burji-Konso Cluster and Borana.[101] There the dates of important public gatherings are publicized; among the far-flung settlements of the Borana, messengers notify people whose presence at them is necessary, and the invitation cannot be refused.[102] As many people as possible should take part in reunions so that the individuals of the community will recognize resolutions as binding without the necessity of coercion.[103]

The opening of an official gathering begins with select elders blessing the participants, and pleading for peace and prosperity. At the All Burji Gatherings, representatives of the scriptural religions utter blessings aloud. Afterward comes an admonition to moderation: interjections are deemed improper, as are standing up during speeches and finger-pointing. Gestures should be reserved and provocations avoided.[104] At large meetings, important legal guidelines are also invoked.[105]

In all places, gatherings require members to be seated, but during large events in Burji, a speaker may stand in order to be heard. As he may not raise himself above others, he directs his words to a "listener" who is also standing and acts as a representative for the others present.

All men whom a matter affects take part in meetings on an equal footing. Each has the right to speak openly, and each should contribute to a decision. In clan and lineage committees as well as among the fuld'o, this includes women too, and at least according to my observations among the Burji-Konso Cluster, they take part energetically and conscientiously. Among the Arsi, women play an important role in negotiations between opposed parties. They also work as ambassadors and informal arbiters in "hot" phases, moving freely between the warring parties, because physical assault on women is prohibited.

After the uttering of the blessings along with reiteration of discussion rules and traditional laws, the dignitary responsible for moderating presents the case at hand. Most often, it is he who has called the meeting to order. He does not preside and is forbidden from swaying others toward a given opinion. He does not exercise authority through the issuance of verdicts. As *princeps inter pares*, he does not sit in judgment, nor does he dictate the results or punishment.

If there is a feud, aggrieved parties may present their sides after the opening ceremony. In legal proceedings, the accused must give an exhaustive version of their arguments, and none may interrupt them or their supporters. There is no institutionalized defense counsel.

Speaker Qualities

Experienced older men who have gained knowledge participating in assemblies enjoy greater influence than others. This is not a gerontocracy, as understanding and expressive capacity rather than age are what is most esteemed. Prestige depends on a person's behavior in assemblies. An uninterested older person counts for little, and young men are meant to learn through participation and also speak, though only if asked. In this way, the younger men develop a capacity for free speech that only a few acquire in our society, and only then through specialized schooling.

Proverbs, short tales, allegories, or historical lore are the most important means of clarifying and dealing with problems. They give vivid expression to situations and, with their basis in oral tradition, broaden the circle of participants figuratively by incorporating ancestors. Adages and traditions help mediation by harmonizing the factual and normative.[106] They do not propose normative claims or instructions for action in the narrow sense but rather set out ethically reflective observations on good and bad behavior.[107] Since their significance (linguistic content) and meaning (semantic content) do not immediately coincide, and meaning depends on application in a given instance, they counteract the ossification of legal norms and impel thought to react flexibly to very different situations.[108] The invocation of proverbs is not at all stereotypical and may convey numerous messages in the course of discussions while also offering reflective potential for traditional motifs to grapple with contemporary reality.[109]

The awareness of proverbs and oral tradition are "cultural capital" that a speaker calls on as a reflective medium in the work of suasion, and are only convincing in political discourses for those acquainted with the community's history, morals, and customs. As the Burji say, "A speech without lore is barren." The Burji prize those who present their standpoint with passion, but when they offend against the principle of consensus and try to put personal interests forward, they meet resistance.[110] A crucial corrective here is the Konso moral concept of truth (*dukaata*), which is closely related to ideals of freedom and upright discussion. In a dispute, truth is an essential part of the order that makes harmony possible.[111]

Participants must respond to manipulations and erroneous opinions, even if with restraint. Often they ignore them, address them indirectly, or combat them with an opposing version that leads the person who put them forth to recognize his error. Provocations and direct reproaches are inevitably avoided to prevent an aggressive discussion climate. In pauses in the assembly, however, heated argument and open criticism are permitted. When conversation grows too intense at an official Borana reunion, an elder will urge calm. If men from the highest Gada grade (*Gaddamoji*) are in attendance, they will start to weep ritually; animosity and aggression then come to an immediate halt. "The assembly remains still and silent until his tears have ceased." Before discussion can go further, prayers restore the disturbed peace.[112]

Speakers reach accord by engaging those present in a kind of dialogue. They will turn to one or several people who will repeat their final words in confirmation, or respond with more or less encouraging interjections. In a number of polycephalic societies, listeners' roles are institutionalized in larger assemblies. The speaker addresses them and receives appropriate feedback, which is refused if he violates prevailing rules. In quarrels, a member of the opposing side acts as listener. He is there to exemplify what the Burji understand by successful communication. The speaker has a right to be heard, and the listener has the duty of listening attentively. He in turn may expect that the speaker will not engage in a monologue and will heed certain rules of discourse.[113]

Reaching Consensus

Especially in the beginning of a dispute, the many repetitions in speakers' addresses are striking. They allow participants to assess the direction that generally acceptable opinion is taking. To clarify matters, as many people as possible should have the chance to speak. The goal of dialogue is to consolidate social harmony, which is expressed through the will to consensus. It is not juristic procedure that dictates the final verdict in legal proceedings; instead, verdicts reflect what has been expressed in the reunion. Like political resolutions, they too must have a basis in consent: a common standpoint reached after weighing diverse opinions, denoting all sides' respect for and acceptance of the solution adopted.

Consensus in judicial proceedings requires that all sides be reconciled.[114] Again, this means restoring the disturbed equilibrium in the community. Proceedings must offer delinquents insight into their guilt. Adults are reminded forcefully of the traditional rules of behavior, and these rules are presented to young people as freely chosen declarations of the people's will. This indoctrination and discourse permit the development of an awareness of wrongdoing that is the condition for comprehension and recognition of their own guilt. Punishment is not a deterrent but rather an expression of insight into the nature of misconduct.

Proceedings can last for days, weeks, or even months, with interruptions. A quick trial by majority rule or decree is impossible. As harmony is essential, no voting procedure exists that would allow one group to defeat another. Interventions are occasionally possible for proceedings that seem to be going nowhere. Dignitaries may admonish assemblies to bring debate to an end. Among the Borana, if consensus appears out of reach, the moderator may break off discussion, but not at his own whim; instead, he must justify his action with reference to the law (aadaa and seera) and relevant precedents. Finally, the assembly must agree with the disruption, again following the logic of consensus.[115]

Verdicts and Pardons

Exhaustive debate in judicial proceedings strives for consensus-based verdicts; verdict and consensus are therefore mutually conditioning. This requires the presentation of the matter at hand and, if necessary, its examination from opposing points of view. In general, approaches to the question of guilt are highly rational. While an oath-taking at a sacred *moora-place* can be called for when suspicion of theft or adultery exists—and on rare occasion, in other cases as well—trial by ordeal is uncommon among the ethnic groups here mentioned. In the Burji-Konso Cluster, though, a seer may participate in exposing the wrongdoer.

Once guilt is established, the gravity and significance of an offense along with its causes are examined in light of the ways that the law has resolved previous cases. Punishment must follow a declaration of guilt, but no compensation is assigned or liability payments made until the parties involved have accepted the verdict. Punishment includes reconciliation through institutionalized forgiveness. Participants expect those on trial to admit their faults, show regret, and request forgiveness publicly. If this occurs, the punishment is drastically reduced, because reconciliation outweighs division and guilty parties should not feel resentment.

Mitigation of punishments, which are initially quite severe, is a common feature of these proceedings and shows two things. First, the committee overseeing the proceedings is permitted to sanction harsh reprisals and is capable of doing so. The trial reflects the community's judgment of the situation and takes the society's goals into account. Second, despite their failings, guilty parties are not excluded. Others want to "reach out to them." For that reason, prudence is considered in the application of norms and mandates.

The reduction of penalties expresses symbolically that excessive zeal in the use of power—above all, if this develops into coercive power—endangers the equality of community members; negotiation always concerns people belonging to one's own community, and they are expected to display insight. If the larger society, as embodied in the committee, places a tolerable check on the use of power against individuals, this sends a signal to individuals that they should restrain their own power in turn and put it into productive use. Should they fail to grasp this signal, society will react with other measures. It is the elders, the very ones entrusted with authority, who exercise this moderating influence. They do not use their potential power to oppress others but instead to facilitate their complete integration into society. Such a proceeding expresses the coupling of societal ideals with the concept and exercise of law.

As soon as the institutional pardon is granted, aggrieved parties must declare their forgiveness publicly. Further enmity will not be tolerated. Forgiveness and acceptance of the punitive measures, followed by the blessing of all present, including the guilty party, bring the proceeding to a close.[116] If people from different religions are present, representatives of each faith will offer blessings and prayers. The accused, now blameless, is reintegrated fully into the community. A common meal normally formalizes the restoration of harmony and social peace. This can include roasted corn, a swig of millet beer, or even the flesh of many oxen.

If proceedings end in this way, a new trial to review the verdict is out of the question. Verdicts reached in common do not produce winners and losers. Common agreement means that no one will look for loopholes in the law to reinterpret the decision to their own benefit.

If, despite thoroughgoing discussion, consensus is unattainable, the *unresolved* case will be referred to a body responsible for broader social unity, such as an interclan committee. This does not signify the revision of a verdict from an "earlier decision" but rather a ruling on a case that extends or threatens to extend beyond those immediately involved to affect broader parts of the society.

The possibility of appeal is characteristic of and meaningful for hierarchical societies. There, a *reduced* elite furnished with higher powers has the right to revise and abrogate lower court decisions. In the Ethiopian monarchies, this was the prerogative of the king or emperor. In polycephalic societies, on the other hand, large gatherings with an *expanded* sociopolitical integration framework are charged with finding solutions benefiting consensus that elude other bodies.

Though less formalized, given the wide variety of often novel questions that they face, committees responding to sociopolitical problems with a particular focus on consensus are not fundamentally different from legal bodies. The stages of the process may be conceived as follows, and generally take place in the following order. In the first step, common values and discussion principles are invoked. Blessings follow, along with reference to communal sentiment and brief remarks on the pending proceedings. In the second step, participants talk about the dangers implied by the matter at hand or its significance for the community, and encourage delinquents to show understanding. If young people are involved, others will take the opportunity to instruct them and sharpen their awareness of the injustice. Guilty parties and their supporters may express themselves freely. The third step is the formulation of a generally acceptable verdict appropriate to the gravity of the offense, and with it, an examination of possible punitive measures. If the guilty party shows understanding and displays regret, a fourth step takes place, with further discussion centered on consensus and the reduction of penalties. Frequently, a speaker will declare the ruling at this point. The fifth step marks the acceptance of this ruling by all present, including the guilty party. The proceedings end with a sixth step that involves a reconciliation ritual, reintegration of the guilty party into society, and finally, the society's blessing.

Excursus: State Law

What is true for the antagonism of the sociopolitical systems in the north and south of present-day Ethiopia is likewise true for their legal systems. For us, what is relevant is first imperial law, then state law after the 1974 revolution, and then their respective application to the colonized.[117] In the south, those overthrown after the conquest lost their laws and land, and were legally bound by their new landlords as serfs (*gabbar*). These landlords had final say over disputes, and "*gabbar* families that collapsed under the burden of peonage were either driven away or killed."[118] Things were not as bad for roaming cattle farming societies, which largely avoided imperial control beyond the requirement of paying tribute for their livestock. Only the balabat, authorized chiefs promoted by the administration, could assign land rights. Things remained this way, save during Italian colonization, until the Ethiopian Revolution and land reform carried out by the Derg in 1975.

The Italian authorities forbid slavery, and the gabbar system ended with the expulsion of the Amharic landlords. The Italians were embraced for their recognition of indigenous courts, to which, according to the Hadiyya, even hunting accidents and crimes resulting in death were transferred after a brief hearing.[119] Rigid state control returned with Haile Selassie. During the Derg regime, kebele organizations replaced the balabats, and kebele courts oversaw justice at the most basic level. Though made up of indigenous party cadres, their structure and power to enforce verdicts (through detention, for example) were a far cry from the practice of the now-proscribed autochthonous legal committees.

Under the monarchy, the colonized retained indigenous law for their internal affairs. Criminal cases were officially the domain of the state judiciary rather than the landlords. Decision-making authority lay with judges instated by the regime, and the emperor was the supreme judge. According to Klausberger, "Autochthonous jurisprudence lost its formal legitimacy, but not its effectiveness. [Local law] thus continued to exist, with the exception ... of blood justice ... largely unbroken outside of state law."[120] Indigenous people got lost in the gears of imperial justice, as I have been told many times, and we have record of the draconian sentences (whippings, severed limbs, being smeared with wax and set afire, etc.) carried out ad hoc after judgment in the shocking images of so-called Ethiopian folk painting.[121] Polycephalic societies, in the face of this brutal violence and hegemony, formed an indissoluble bond; for them, intergroup violence is unacceptable, and not even an indigenous court may mandate it. Violence is only legitimate in war, where it may be desirable in the face of unrelenting enemy violence. As a consequence, authorities that exercise violence are also hostile; they place the society in a state of war, which it is always proper to avoid. It is true that those sentenced in state courts are no longer mutilated, but prison sentences, torture, and the death penalty are equally unacceptable.

Especially when punishments were carried out immediately, state courts deliberately let quarreling parties' aggression run its course and then would provide plaintiffs with their officially sanctioned, state-controlled redress. The proceedings of committee courts in polycephalic societies strive to defuse aggression both ad hoc and sustainably throughout the trial. Their reconciliation politics aims for a shared future, and the conscientious avoidance of draconian punishments in their legal system is an active expression of will meant to forestall hegemony in the social and political realms.

Transformations in the Legal System

Since the Ethiopian Revolution of 1974, and especially after 1994, when the constitution passed following the fall of the

Derg formally recognized the indigenous justice system, a positive tendency toward legal pluralism has gathered force.[122] But indigenous people still harbor significant resentment toward the state judicial system. This is a product primarily of their sense of helplessness—undoubtedly drawn from experience—vis-à-vis court verdicts, along with the knowledge that these have been biased and at times influenced by corruption.[123] Other important factors include experiences with changes in government and the associated value conceptions propagated by the state. There is also is the widespread awareness of the state's role in undermining indigenous institutions through hegemonic interventions in the territories aimed at altering and weakening the traditional legal system.

In parallel, revitalization attempts have gathered strength, as in the aforementioned debate over the restitution of the office of woma, and these, along with external pressures, have kept the discussion of legal conceptions alive. Polycephalic societies in the Horn of Africa clearly trust their own legal system, which is legitimated by its communitarian makeup and application as a part of lived reality, and has proven itself a reliable, sustainable alternative to state law throughout political and ideological vicissitudes.

Highly significant are the changes in the adaption of the law to the All Borana Gathering (*guumii gaayoo*) that takes place every eight years. There, legal *norms* are subject to alteration in the course of time, but legal *processes*, and in particular the manner of negotiation, show continuity without stagnation. This is a manifestation of cognitive as well as practical strength working to counteract hegemonic ambitions despite political changes in Ethiopia, Kenya, and Somalia—not always successfully, as developments in northern and southern Somalia show. Still, in regions surrounding larger cities, conflict resolution procedures survive even when awareness of indigenous legal systems is scanty.[124]

III.5. CONSIDERATIONS ON THE ACCEPTANCE OF DECISIONS

Foreign travelers and ethnologists remain astonished at how resolutions and verdicts are reached, accepted, and enforced without physical violence or an executive body. The very question of how that which is recognized as right may be implemented was an intractable and frantically debated problem for theoreticians of anarchism around 1900. Naturally, severe penalties exist in polycephalic societies for those who disregard committees' decisions, but these are only valid for serious transgressions, usually involving repeat offenders, and are the exception rather than the rule.

When I asked people from southern Ethiopian polycephalic societies forced to pay compensation whether they would have preferred to forgo it, or had complied only to avoid further trouble, they reacted with incomprehension; in the end, people had come together in mutual understanding—in consensus. The matter was done with, and the person himself fully integrated into the community; payment was therefore a matter of course.[125]

Fear of ostracism may be involved, but it is not an essential motive. This is easier to understand if one keeps in mind that striving for peace is both an elementary concern of polycephalic societies and a condition for the maintenance of nonhegemony. Accordingly, enmity is to be avoided as a rule. This is a difficult aim to achieve, but East African polycephalic societies have integrated conflict potential structurally: there is a complementary arrangement of important societal institutions, from the lineage system with parallel lines and heritable offices, to the territorial associations, generation group system, and societally desirable associations of personal networks. These make equilibrium possible, though hardly inevitable; after all, these individual domains fulfill distinct social functions that include antagonistic group interests and personal preferences. This array of fields with their different orientations is a precondition for a polycephalic form of socialization. Only a multitude of contradictory interests can produce a diversity of power relations opposed to centralization and requiring constant recalibration.

Inevitably, the individual adult male who belongs to numerous institutions faces a difficult dilemma. Every person must confront, along with ordinary problems, those arising within and among institutions, but the demand for an executive to offer and enforce solutions would contradict the basic principles of polycephalic societies. Conflicts must and should be examined as well as resolved among equal parties to prevent the destabilization of the society. Indeed, moderation through institutions strengthens a society's coherence because unsustainable structures may be transformed creatively and innovations integrated.[126]

Heuristically, we can distinguish between sociopolitical and juristic inquiries, but frequently these flow together in practice when seeking the best path toward social harmony. And the different communities agree broadly on the nature of communicative action in dealing with both sorts of proceedings. In view of the breadth of inquiries that they address, we may view them as arenas of cultural maintenance and formation that reflect, and if necessary actuate, social relations while working through antagonisms creatively and in a participative manner. This can open up new perspectives that encourage modified cultural manifestations so that norms and conceptions handed down by ancestors concerning the proper conduct of life may be reconciled with the conditions and demands of the present. Discourse manifests the close relations between egalitarian ethics, the polycephalic social order, and the establishment of norms.

Reflections on the individual mode of life are anchored in the traditions of the Burji and Dullay, if we take the idea of the unfinished creation to relate metaphorically to the first people who "forged" the first institutions and the wisdom of emulating them. People must sustain and push forward the process of creation, which has no telos of its own. The established order demands transformation to keep it alive. Traditions are not dogma but rather thought models that may be construed in numerous ways. What Bénézet Bujo describes as "African ethics" is also valid here: to create a sustainable future, discourses are open to reflection within the individual tradition and reception of other experiences from outside that tradition.[127]

Polycephalic societies recognize the importance of discourse for stabilizing society; their assemblies strictly regulate proceedings and the behavior of speakers while stressing the value of truth seeking. Listener feedback exercises a control function, and persistent attention is demanded. Exhaustive discussions are permitted, but must address a reality perceptible to all, neither veering off into self-presentation nor deviating from the theme. During assemblies, power differences among disputants are set aside, and each participant must show respect for the others. Among the Sidaama, for example, before taking the floor, one must ask the previous speaker for permission.[128]

A speaker's truthfulness is especially prized, and assemblies inevitably devote a great deal of time to the search for truth.[129] The moral conception of truth is tightly allied with ideals of peace and upright conversation. An argument may claim validity when it hews to truth and socially recognized norms—as with Jürgen Habermas, who defines the validity of claims for discourse as propositional truth, normative correctness, and subjective truthfulness.[130] This means first that the substance of the matter to be discussed must be clear, and no speaker may adduce an argument unrelated to the subject. Second, the speaker accepts this norm and therefore has a claim to reflect on it. And third, the speaker means what he says.

Habermas's demands are also cornerstones of discussion in the assemblies examined here. This is not a matter of abstract philosophical concepts but of relations to reality, veracity, and the sincerity of the speaker. Sincerity is a condition for inner-societal peace and the stability of the community, and is finally significant as an antithesis to the lie: hence, the semantic field of the Burji word *labbee*—lie— includes not only an intentionally uttered falsehood, as in Western cultures, but slander, betrayal, and fighting words. It further encompasses any use of speech that may have destructive consequences for human life in common.[131]

Respected elders chosen for this purpose oversee the organization, procedural transparency, and moderation of official sessions, while themselves possessing neither executive power nor means of coercion by which to enforce decisions. They are assigned power to assure that discussion cleaves to the society's concerns and posited norms. But this is not a power *over* persons or institutions. Instead, this form of power, which requires astuteness in judgment, may be understood, following Arendt, as authority. It is assignable to persons and demands, not compulsion or suasion, but rather respect. Its opposite is not enmity but contempt or scorn, such as befell a formerly recognized authority figure in Sidama.[132]

Authority is constantly on trial. This provision hinders the misuse of power and is one of the stabilizing features of polycephalic societies. The power of the officiant (the leader and moderator in a discussion) is exposed to the opposing power of the assembly, which for its part assures that the officiant upholds the values he represents. At large Borana assemblies, the specific education of the hayyuu gives them the authority to speak up for the purpose of reaching consensus, but not for exercising power. This kind of education is the exception in polycephalic societies, where any married man can moderate so long as he shows interest in his society and exhibits that engagement that in principle is expected of all. He can and should make his own—as cultural and social capital in Pierre Bourdieu's sense—that knowledge of his own culture and of assembly procedures that he acquires through participation and interactions with experienced elders. The society treasures this capital, which a speaker may use to lend weight to his words in a gathering. After reaching a suitable age, if he has exhibited selflessness, he can presume to be recommended as a moderator.

A necessary contradiction is embedded in the implementation of authority as in these partly antagonistic institutions. The community's dilemma lies in its need for engaged, active, creative, and ambitious personalities who must be hindered from using their authority for selfish ends. As leaders may only employ words as political action—and even here, not monopolistically—and are incorporated into the reigning system of norms, a synthesis of antagonisms takes place in the assemblies that drives discourse forward.

The allusion to the unfinished creation along with the consequent imperative to work *with* and above all *on* traditions does not in the least mean that mythical thinking imprisons these societies, or that they are incapable of rational decisions. Yet this is precisely what Habermas asserts when he denies developed rationality to these societies and affirms that they are capable only of dogmatic statements.

The untenability of his thesis is clear in the Burji-Konso Cluster, where the semantic field of the "reasonable" proceeds from the ironbound correlation between knowledge, wisdom, probity, sincerity, and responsibility.[133] John Hamer discovered that the strict rules for conduct in gatherings among the Sidama in the southwest of Ethiopia were the very thing that made pragmatic discussion possible. Common belief in the ideals of truth and sincerity form the basis of rational discourse as employed in conflict resolution and political proceedings—and their reliance on truth claims and a normative relation to situational understanding are comparable to the premises for rational discourse that Habermas stipulates.[134]

The Sidama and Barotse do refer to mythical aspects of historicizing tales if the search for applicable norms in a given case proves fruitless. One should not underestimate these tales' significance: Western concepts of rationality and logic are not the only path to socially relevant resolutions. Balinese mythical traditions also possess reflexive efficacy, and if it is true that Burji oral traditions retain wholly mythical elements, these are not readily invoked as dogmatic statements governing the understanding of the world; instead, they offer models for thinking adapted to a variety of applications.[135] Tradition is not a means for collective subjugation beneath an overarching body of thought but rather a medium promoting the development of new lines of discussion. Connected to the familiar, yet turning a critical eye to it, tradition sensibly brings inherited cultural elements into contact with the modern.

A striking characteristic of the dialogue forms employed in assemblies is their will to unity, to consensus, which is itself a precondition for collective action. A democratic majority that leaves outvoted losers behind is unknown in these proceedings. This is true not only for the polycephalic societies examined here but for other sub-Saharan African populations too. The Arusha, for instance, "talk and talk" until they have reached agreement, and set no store by neutral arbiters.[136] They will always settle a matter among themselves.[137]

The West African philosopher Kwasi Wiredu derives his theory of consensus ethics from African examples and joins it to a plea for a nonpartisan politics.[138] In *The Human Condition* and other writings, Arendt examined the interrelation with others in speaking and action.[139] Through language, actions are coordinated and steered into ordered paths. Collective communication with acknowledgment of the other can evolve into politically relevant action serving conviviality without coercion.

Analogies can be drawn between the process and aims of the discourses discussed here and Habermas's theory of communicative action and the discourse ethics that he developed in 1973 with Karl-Otto Apel. One may not expect complete congruence; among other things, African and western European conceptions have divergent goals. One seeks the solution of concrete problems that arise in practice, while the other attempts to ground a universal claim in theory on the basis of philosophical observations.[140] Nonetheless, comparison is meaningful even if it does not mean translating imported thoughts and actions into my own conceptual tradition. A knowledge of discourse ethics has been enlightening for my understanding of my subject societies' discussion forums, giving me a window through which to view certain phenomena. These two German philosophers take their considerations to be an extension of the European Enlightenment by means of communication theory. Consequently, Immanuel Kant's maxim that man is an end in himself, in which freedom and reason are dialectically bound together, is valid for them. This conception of the subject forms the epistemological fundament of the Enlightenment and is a principle with claims to universal validity, one that not even the UN Charter on Human Rights has failed to take account of. Discourse ethics also presupposes that autonomous, self-responsible subjects must be able to act and communicate free from compulsion.

None other than Foucault called into question the ostensible universality of the autonomous subject, describing the history of its origin as the product of heterogeneous historical events—particularly societal power practices and their constellations, which exerted an influence on people's thoughts and actions (see section II.2). Keeping in mind this historicity and the culturally specific configuration of modern Western subjectivity, a comparison of the European concept of discourse ethics and discourse as realized in polycephalic societies is invalid; distinct, historically grounded ideas of the person lie at the base of each. In polycephalic societies, a person should stand before their fellow people autonomously, aware of their responsibility in society. This is not the same as being absorbed into the collective. To the contrary, adults should show strength of character, courage, engagement, and a capacity to offer well-grounded judgments on social and political questions.[141] Still, Bourdieu's concept of the habitus, whereby the patterns of perception, behavior, and thought acquired through socialization are reflected and internalized, is applicable to individuals' scope of action in these societies. This finite reservoir, shaped by social conditions, structures but does not determine social practice. Actors are restrained by their habitus, but free to develop strategies across a variety of societal planes.[142]

Despite numerous differences between Western and African thinking, there are parallels and points of intersection. Indeed, the affinities are significant in formal discourse procedure, which is among Habermas's key points of emphasis. The binding rules cited previously (section II.5), which according to Habermas are meant to guarantee participants' equality of opportunity, are equivalent to those stressed in gatherings in polycephalic societies. Habermas further establishes theoretical connections likewise valid for communication techniques in polycephalic societies: the possibility of understanding is the common lifeworld of all participants, and it preserves the experiences of previous generations, which are sources for the interpretation of contemporary problems.[143] The cooperative production of convictions against the background of the individual worldview is acceptable to all members, and enables them to recognize new connections of meaning and strive for appropriate social action. A corollary is the evocation of discourses on value and questions of ethics, which in turn may lead—if necessary—to the transformation of norms and instatement of new legal principles. Engagement in such discourse, carried out in common through free reflection, must be perceived, especially in anarchic societies, as a community-building force, even if Habermas would disagree. Here, Arendt's concept of "communicative power" is germane. In polycephalic societies and consensually realized institutions, it offers to all those concerned with the common good a power that remains effective so long as the communicative action of participatory democracy (Arendt's term) keeps it alive. It protects political freedom, as Habermas underscores, "in resistance against the forms of repression that threaten political liberty internally or externally."[144] Societies forfeit this freedom not only when they have ceased to be sovereign over communicative action (and consequently, the establishment of norms), or state power has restricted this power or stripped it away entirely, but also when they give it up of their own accord.[145] The Horn of Africa provides more than enough examples here.

For committees' labor in society to be recognized, their functional capacity must be guaranteed and made visible. Committees' stability guarantees the security of the law, and so it is important that as many people as possible participate, and elders are obliged to contribute responsibly. Evasions of this obligation detract from the prestige of gatherings, which are always public, as well as for the law, which they represent. With legal pluralism prevailing in African states, the situation of traditional law is often precarious enough, and dependent on changing power relations. But particularly in southern Ethiopia, frequent fluctuations in the country's regime and its associated ideologies have led to populations in many places trusting traditional law over state law.

III.6. ESTABLISHMENT OF CONSENSUS: RATIONAL COMMUNICATION AND SENSORY EXPERIENCE

Both the Western concept of communicative action and the exhaustive discussions in assemblies examined here aim for mutually agreed-on solutions to pending problems. Analogies, however, should not wipe away all differences. The previously cited African philosophers Bujo and Kwasi Wiredu see defining features of African concepts above all in the question of goals to be pursued through resolutions that all can agree on as well as the influence this has on associated processes. The key concept here is consensus.

In polycephalic societies, consensus preserves social peace. It is, though, something more than a compromise between conflicting interests for the sake of which discrepancies are set aside. Well-considered insights, assessed through argumentation, are required, along with the readiness to sacrifice one's own point of view in favor of comprehensively grounded considerations. Time is set aside for careful reflection to avoid the pressure to conform. Only those convinced of the sensibleness and morally justifiable correctness of, for instance, a new provision, and thus able to adopt it as a principle, will form part of a consensus.

For Habermas, too, agreement based on fleeting impressions or presumed certainties is insufficient. Discursively generated consensus must come from rationally motivated agreement for the norms generated in order to achieve validity. The individual must overcome their subjective conception and integrate others' standpoint into their own thinking (what Arendt calls "reflective judgment").

According to Kwasi Wiredu, compromise becomes consensus when none perceive it as unacceptable. Individuals may not fully agree with the proposal under debate, but may accede to it in order to restore harmony in the interest of a stable community. It suffices that "all parties have the feeling that their viewpoint regarding a suggested plan for future action or conviviality has received adequate consideration."[146] Anke Graneß sees the goal less as the realization of abstract justice than the reconciliation of opposed interests.[147] For Graeber, too, consensus is not complete agreement but rather a process that "at least in that minimal sense [ensures] malcontents can still feel they have freely chosen to go along with bad decisions."[148]

In many respects, practice in polycephalic societies is nearer Habermas's discourse ethics that Kwasi Wiredu's consensus ethics, which draws by and large on West African examples. In polycephalic societies, every person is a *zoon politikon*, so more than mere passive agreement is expected from discussion participants (and more than mentioned in Graeber as well). While consensus ethics demands that individuals occasionally stifle themselves for the good of society, in polycephalic societies, the justification of points of view is at issue. As in Habermas's discourse ethics, in polycephalic societies it is essential that "normative claims to validity have a cognitive meaning and can be treated *as* truth claims."[149] Yet claims to universal truth do not exist in polycephalic societies. Instead, they recognize, in Foucault's words, an "ensemble of rules according to which the true and the false are separated and specific effects of power attached to the true."[150]

Consensus in polycephalic societies has an immediate, practical relation to the harmonization of society along with the justification of values and norms. This places its conception squarely in the African context. Discourse ethics and the theory of communicative action refrain from such concrete goal setting, restricting themselves to formal principles.[151] Even where Habermas differentiates between universal significance discourse (which arrives at universal norms) and lifeworld-based application discourse, "application discourses [remain] with the principle of suitability ... still on the plane of theory, even if they are in opposition to justification theory relevant to facts and situations."[152]

In polycephalic societies, discussions offer moral orientation for objectively relevant action where the success of human existence is key. The avoidance of false compromises here is completely valid. As Habermas has shown in his look at application discourse, agreement does not necessarily preclude falsehood (see above), which only a suitable process avoids, to the extent that such is possible. The conscious pursuit of suitable solutions and intersubjective validity, taking into account as many points of view and new insights as possible, can last for months. Critical confrontation with normative claims and discussion rules is essential, as is the holistic conception of the person, who is always perceived in polycephalic societies in a broad social, temporal, and cosmic frame of reference. This opposes perspectives and modes of action that arise solely from individual interest, or might have deleterious effects on future generations.

In contrast to Habermas, what matters here are not rules for universal correctness but rather the promotion of good practice over bad in concrete situations. This is evident in just a few words from the opening speech of the court gatherings described above: "We, who are constantly liable to the good, we, who constantly avoid the bad, we discuss together how we work out our life in common."

Consensus-based (and for that reason, socially recognized) ethically oriented laws are thus more directive than imperative. Insofar as they express the power of the many, drawing the largest possible number of viewpoints into juridical and political decisions, in contrast to authoritarian societies, they curb the misuse and monopolization of power, and as such are critical counterweights to hegemony in polycephalic and anarchistic societies.[153]

The danger that consensus may allow the passage of measures harmful to society or individuals seems to loom, above all, in the confrontation with the "modern," because those affected can hardly grasp adequately the global influences at play and in turn have no influence on them. The danger appears graver for the economy and politics than for the judicial realm.

As opposed to the discourse ethics of Apel and Habermas, ethics in polycephalic societies, with its specific conceptions of the right and good life, does not raise a claim to a universally valid schema appropriate to a multitude of lifeways. Instead, it presents a plausible claim to rationality, oriented toward concrete situations, for those socialized in a similar way. Discourse should give rise to a common basis with common relations to meaning, offering the possibility of substantial social integration.

As is evident from the legal procedures treated here, consensus embraces even feuding parties and those that the community has found guilty; indeed, it is important that the latter acknowledge their misdeeds. Atonement directs the consensual verdict toward reintegration and the restoration of social harmony. Parties to a conflict acknowledge their failings and may be reconciled with the community; the verdict is more compromise than punishment.[154] Delinquents, like the ill, are not left alone with their problems. Edification and punishment are conscientious actions intended to reveal to feuding parties their shared responsibility. At issue is not only the restoration of harmony and community but also mutual obligation as a condition for a life in common that benefits all. Here we can glimpse a form of East African responsibility ethics.

What is demanded is reintegration through rituals that accompany the positing of laws and attainment of consensus while stressing the human and cosmic orders, which must be restored to equilibrium. Though a broad ethnological literature examining rituals exists, it has unfortunately led to their disparagement as an irrational, pseudojuridical activity of "primitive societies" imprisoned in mystical thinking (this perspective is also visible in Habermas). But rituals do not exist to the detriment of law; instead, they lend emphasis to the verbal on a physically perceptible plane. The ethnic groups treated here do not engage blindly in "meaningless rites" (Adolf Ellegard Jensen); rather, their ceremonies promote understanding of the other and produce generally accepted guidelines for behavior. Rituals confirm and sanction decisions, as their performative nature highlights.[155] Cult practices imbue the publicly expressed contract, which all now recognize, with a binding character. And ritually assumed obligations give their participants assurances for the future.

Following Victor Turner's research into ritual, another point of view is worth mentioning: at the end of strained conflict mediation proceedings, rituals may present a safety valve for aggrieved parties by allowing volatile emotional states to be effectively expressed.

Sacred transfiguration and the rituals it implies also characterize Western law with its commitment to the *ratio*: an atmosphere of cultic reverence reigns in the courtroom, and proceedings there are strictly ritualized. Judges and attorneys wear robes; the public rises at the beginning and end of the session, and may not eat, drink, or smoke. Court-room and everyday behavior are distinguished in the same way that ritual distinguishes sacred from profane. The symbols employed—the statue of blind justice or image of Moses with the tablets of the law—belong to the ritual domain. Even the form of some court buildings, which resemble Greek temples, makes clear their relation to the sacred; such is the case of the US Supreme Court. The ambience and proceedings evince a desire to bring the legal civic order and cosmic one into correspondence.[156]

The sacred is always bound up with power, and African examples too confirm the bond between ritual and displays of power. The integration of the supernatural makes resolutions binding and reinforces a gathering's decision-making capacities. But here the law grants reconciliation, because guilt is ritually annulled. In the Christian West, the sovereign's monopoly on violence lacks this moment of reconciliation. Mediation is a recent phenomenon that may stand in for proper legal proceedings, but is only stipulated for a limited number of cases.

In polycephalic societies, rituals are intimately bound up with the quelling of discord so as to prevent the resort to violence. A remarkable illustration is a peace meeting that brought together twelve ethnic groups after years of bloody conflict in the region north of Lake Chew Bahir. The meeting was above all an opportunity for representatives to declare their wish for peace to each other. Not only arguments, but also rituals played a central role here.

Only rituals enacted in common—gift exchange, burial of weapons, the cursing of discord and war, and especially blessings, always accompanied by group singing—managed to establish common ground, reinforcing the bonds of the ethnic groups present while giving form to the agreements and resolutions reached.[157]

Accord is only possible when the will to agreement exists and animosities can be set aside. The artificial space of ritual presents participants with the opportunity to abandon the quotidian space of enmity, and step into a sphere "where dissension and disruption is cognitively and affectively hard to imagine."[158] Those involved succeed in resolving conflicts and dispatching problems by their own strength, *without* the superordinate authority of the state, which has proven itself chronically incapable of mitigating ethnic conflicts.

* * *

In polycephalic societies, consensus is the collective generation and acknowledgment of a decision. The communicative norms it reflects are implemented and followed, first because those affected recognize and admit them, and second, because they have manifestly incorporated them through rituals that encompass all participants.

Key stages in juridical proceedings are compensation for damages and rehabilitation of the offender, who understands the consequences of their actions. But the binding of consensus and ritual also aids in the prevention of conflicts, inasmuch as proceedings strive for peace between people or groups (or at least for the reduction of social tension) along with the harmonization of a society in which there should be no losers. No one must bow to a majority resolution, as in the Western democratic model. Resolutions are followed voluntarily rather than from fear of sanction. Rooted in understanding, they are self-obligatory and dispense with any coercive apparatus.[159]

"Modern" legal systems, in contrast, rest on the (exemplary) punishment of offenders, separating them from the community and locking them in prison. The threat of punishment should frighten the potential wrongdoer, leading to a change of orientation and personal betterment, but for inmates, the essential lesson is not to be caught next time. Recently, the problem of reintegration into society has received more attention, but resocialization programs have not affected the demand for subordination, which is a basic characteristic of the state.

Local jurisprudence in southern Ethiopia—with its communicatively reflected legal norms—can withstand the competition of state jurisdiction in those places where communities cultivate anarchic values. Even without implementational authority, it holds a strong position in the context of legal pluralism because the verdicts of state courts have no capacity to offer social security to the affected parties.

IV THE LEGAL COMMUNITY AS GUARANTOR OF NONHEGEMONIC SOCIETY

The foregoing chapters demonstrate that in their dealings with social and legal problems, the conceptions and practices of polycephalic societies are opposed to hegemonic structures. But to what extent do legal conceptions and practices support the principles of polycephalic life in common? Can they guarantee community cohesion? And what does it mean for a society when the capacity for reaching consensus or verdicts within the community proves elusive or is disputed?

Rainer Neu's inquiries into the history of Israel offer essential insights into the interconnection of legal and social developments.[1] Referring to Old Testament texts and ethnological research, he analyzes the premonarchical Israelite society of the eleventh century before Christ as a segmentary autonomous legal and religious community with patrilineal kinship ties. It had no "juristic-systematic ambition," but rather strove to preserve equilibrium within the society through arbitration.[2] In the course of subsequent social developments, kinship tribunals gave rise to a far-reaching community tribunal incorporating every full citizen. There were no judges, and legislative and executive functions coincided with the autonomous regional lay jurisdiction.

With the advent of monarchy, the legal system was centralized, though at first, monarchical jurisdiction did not impend on the competencies of the local one. Even in the time of David and Solomon in the tenth century BC, officialdom still counted no judges among its ranks. With the later establishment of a state judicial system, "free citizens lost their sovereignty in the lay courts" and "the last institutional refuge of anarchic tradition fell victim to the monarchy's will to centralization."[3] According to Neu, the men endowed with full rights did not accept this curtailment of their political right to legislate and the consequent harm to their social status without resistance. This explains the uprisings and scorn of the prophets who admonish the state courts. Examples can be found in Amos (5.12), which notes that "they afflict the just, they take a bribe, and they turn aside the poor in the gate *from their right*," and in Isaiah (10.1): "Woe unto them that decree unrighteous decrees, and that write grievousness *which* they have prescribed; to turn aside the needy from judgment, and to take away the right from the poor of my people, that widows may be their prey, and *that* they may rob the fatherless!" The legitimate application of the law—and not overt violence—brought the people into dependency and need, and justice became an instrument for exploitation and hegemony. The enforcement of state justice "must be seen as the final victory of ambition for political centralization over the principle of segmentation, which forever vanished as a structural feature of societies in Israel/Juda."[4]

Similarly suggestive is the evolution of the Oromo groups, which took possession of a region that stretched from the northern border of the Kingdom of Kaffa to today's

Wollega in the eighteenth century. In contrast to regions lying further west and north, where the Oromo retained their polycephalic social order after the conquest campaigns and assimilated the subjugated populations, after just one hundred years, seven Oromo states had arisen in the disputed area, and were frequently described in their totality as Gibe states.

In the region known as Jimma, on the Kaffa frontier, the Oromo established a confederation not long after the conquest that was bound together by an oath (*kaka*). Contacts among the confederated Oromo factions were reduced to gatherings (*čaffee*) to which all Gadda groups sent their representatives. The čaffee were centered on legal questions and common legislation, just as in other Oromo groups.[5] But as conflicts among the factions increased, a number of elected military leaders managed to successfully expand their competencies.[6] Oral tradition states that the first tendencies toward centralization came with the election of the army leader Abbaa Faaroo at the end of the eighteenth century. Faaroo established "law and order" in the land; the čaffee committee was not in the position to do so because it possessed no means to enforce its resolutions. He is also said to have imposed taxes and compulsory labor in contrast to traditional egalitarian principles.[7]

When the Capuchin Wilhelm Massija stayed in Jimma in 1854, he reported that only a few years before, there had been ten different groupings of warlords struggling with each other. In those years, there was evidently (still) no effective central authority.[8] Massija witnessed the dwindling of the influence of the čaffee and their incapacity to enforce their decisions concerning the conflicts among the war-lords. [9] The Gada committees became drastically weaker with the ruling class's conversion to Islam in 1830. This enabled kings to break with tradition and the sacred order of the Gada system, and legitimize the reign of their dynastic line. The king appointed himself supreme justice, and revision of his decisions was impossible. Legal entities and official posts were organized hierarchically. Influential and rich citizens bent the law to their will, and bribery became key to winning cases. [10]

The kings of Gibe, particularly the leaders of Jimma, did not abide by restrictions and rituals like the sacral kings of southern Ethiopia, and their potential for violence was such that they may reasonably be called despots. [11] Even if the elders' assembly still existed in Jimma up to the twentieth century, its influence was only narrow, and with the introduction of Islamic law it lost its legislative powers. [12]

While the historical processes are different, the Gibe states offer important analogies to much earlier developments in Israel. These include the emergence of rival warlords who based their legitimacy on threats from without: in Israel, the Philistines, and among the Oromo, the Abyssinian Kingdom. In both instances, wealth acquired from control of trade routes favored the exercise of hegemony, which along with the suppression of basic democratic institutions, allowed for the growth of centralization. The Gibe states also confirm that when a society is stripped of the self-regulating capacity that arises from communication, the community of legal persons as a refuge for autonomy inevitably dissolves.[13] This represents the triumph of centralized hegemony over anarchic or polycephalic society—but not the disappearance of the idea of an egalitarian community. New impulses may always recur in society's interstices.

Also worth noting is that the urge toward centralization did not encompass all Oromo groups. Therefore, this was not an inevitable evolutionary process. Many Oromo communities have retained their polycephalic social orders up to the present day. To prevent its collapse, they consciously keep their basic conception of law through sociopolitical discourse, like other societies in the Horn of Africa. Their awareness is sharpened through their relations with neighboring ethnic groups as well as experiences with the state's monopoly on force based on law. The legal pluralism now recognized by the state enables them to practice their own law, which they recognize as a shelter for their polycephalic anarchic societal order.

*   *   *

In polycephalic societies, the community actively takes part in the configuration of values, and an internalization of the concept of freedom takes place in the social and political framework. Legal and moral conceptions along with their reflection in free communication are an essential component of these people's lifeworld, and at the same time leave a decisive mark on their habitus. The habitus is both the productive basis of societal relations and their outcome, and an unbroken back and forth exists between the two (see section III.5).

In the polycephalic societies examined here, communal life impregnates a variety of social sectors and domains that are not hierarchically organized or structured, but also do not merely stand side by side as equivalents. They should be conceived of as a rhizome, which allows for different situational adaptations. Consequently, the translation of ethical conceptions and societal ideals into patterns of behavior and norms is fluid and not directed. If the community considers it meaningful, then norms may be transformed into legal rules.

For the positing of values, as for the administration of justice, people work in common, with equal rights, through free communication. For participants, this leads to an attitude of libertarian opposition to any form of paternalism. The societally recognized power accorded to committees and those working within them supports this attitude.

Conceptions of crime, theft, deception, murder, and so on are largely comparable in our law and that of polycephalic societies. In many cases, notions of their respective gravity differ only slightly. If one considers the legal corpus as an independent domain, with only indirect relationships to other branches of society—and in this way, cordoned off from its specifically social implications—it is not initially recognizable as a hegemonic or nonhegemonic instrument. But there are major differences from the legal codices of hegemonically regulated societies, among others, in terms of judgments concerning the misuse of power or position. There are also cases where a greater degree of gravity is observable, as in the incest prohibition and its expansion.

Different, too, is the application of law to delinquents: in polycephalic societies, stress is laid not on punishment but instead reconciliation.

In essence, however, the handling of legal cases in polycephalic and centralized social orders is diametrically opposed. This is true from the outset for the legally ensured communication structure among persons of equal rights that is common to polycephalic societies. In discussions of situationally extrapolated "positive law," they stress resistance to hegemony, which would destroy the communicative structure. Avoidance of power discrepancies extends to the formulation of verdicts and even the sentencing of social misconduct. The quintessence of African traditional law lies not in the regulation of the branches of the law but rather in the way cases are discussed and resolved; this vital difference from European law, which also is valid for polycephalic societies, was only brought to light by legal ethnologists in the 1950s.[14] Antony Allott, Andrew Epstein, and Max Gluckman came to this conclusion examining the legal system of the traditional kingdom of the Rotse—in other words, a hierarchical society. In addition to this, the rejection of accumulation of possessions must be emphasized; further, great importance lies in the way power relations are apportioned among discussants and what ethos underlies the legal judgments.

Antihegemonic patterns arise in legally safeguarded communication among equals, but we may not suppose that these *alone* suffice to implement antihegemonic praxis. Far more essential to the incorporation of the sociopolitical nonhegemonic model is the *interplay* of law, institutions, and social-relational systems, because existing institutions on their own may have only limited capability for curtailing hegemony.

Regulations in force for individual institutions are no guarantee of a thriving polycephalic society because there, too, equilibrated relations are necessary. Just as significant for their effectiveness, if not more so, is that these institutions be filled with life, redeveloped and reframed, to stave off the danger that they will ossify, and their intended results be translated into their opposite. To preserve the vitality of institutions, a vigilant confrontation with contemporary questions is necessary, and along with it, measures and rules negotiated hand in hand with assemblies. These rules are not inflexible laws but instead rules of play, as it were, for the political. They activate the freedom to employ power on the part of the many and curb its misuse.

The internalization of the sociopolitical liberatory (anti-hegemonic) framework and the interpenetration of distinctive spheres is illustrated in the model displayed here. Movement in this model should be understood as circular, traveling in clockwise and counterclockwise directions.

Different institutions with their structurally antagonistic relationships stand in equilibrium, and are cognitively bound with the societally and religiously sanctioned legal complex. The relationship between the law and societal institutions is established through different assemblies whose scope can stretch from the clan to the entire ethnic group—and this linkage lends a particular sociopolitical significance to

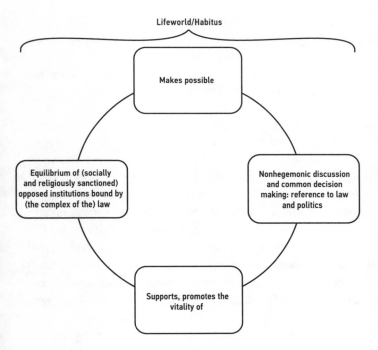

the law in polycephalic societies. This constellation, which already embraces an antipaternalistic attitude in its individual institutions and people, *makes possible* nonhegemonic conversation, its influence on the law and politics. The order of communicative action employed for the goal of consensus in different committees *sustains* these institutions with their immanent contradictions and fills them with life as well as maintaining the institutional reciprocity that society requires. In parallel, their communicative style presupposes a nonhegemonic social constitution: social organization and conflict resolution condition one another mutually in a legal society of engaged actors. This is key for our understanding of political, social, and legal conduct in polycephalic societies.

The reciprocal, partly antagonistic bonds between institutions and their connection with the law discourage ambition among upstarts, and inhibit the predominance of any given societal domain. This constellation thus acts as a counterpower to the internal striving for sovereignty and the hegemony of the state. Resistance to centralization and state paternalism with its monopoly on power is not carried out through armed violence in polycephalic societies.[15] Instead, successful creation of autonomous local spaces depends on a commonly held anarchic disposition and the people's will to preserve all this through their own laws.

Many readers may have the impression that my explanations offer an idealistic image of polycephalic societies in particular and human behavior in general. We should, though, allow that there do exist societies where paradigms other than our own are valid—ones where the isolation of the individual has not gone so far as in Western societies. Ones where profit maximization is not the highest value, and where competitive behavior always respects the dignity of others.

Polycephalic societies may serve as a pattern, if not an ideal type, of the mode of functioning for highly populous anarchic communities. They show that even without a monopoly on violence, societal action, legal security, and internal peace are possible. For this, interactions with the law are essential.

Thus, case studies of nonhegemonic conviviality in southern Ethiopia have significance far beyond the Horn of Africa. They offer an interpretative framework that describes nonhegemonic societies in a universalizing way, clarifying the interdependencies and causal relations among their significant features. Clearly the described models cannot simply be carried over to other societies—and certainly not to our own—but they can open new perspectives. In any case, numerous tendencies toward the creation of egalitarian modes of conduct also exist in the West.

In the critique of existing hierarchical leadership forms based on violence, theoreticians of anarchism of the nineteenth and twentieth centuries developed ideal models for a future stateless society, where humanity and equality would reign. How feasible this is remains a matter for discussion. Education and voluntary cooperation show some promise. But what if the privileged do not want to give up their prerogatives? Should pressure be applied? The resort to violence inevitably conceals the danger that new hegemonic relationships will arise; Western anarchists found themselves constantly ensnared in this dilemma, given their historical circumstances. The short-term failure of anarchic societies in reality long made it easy for their opponents to banish the idea of nonhegemonic society to the realm of utopia.

Yet that should not be taken to mean that the modern concept of the state, permeated by capitalist ideology, as a global sociopolitical panacea is valid. In the face of existing—and functioning—"societies without the state," the fixation on statehood, which retains its status as a credible guarantor of inner as well as outer security despite the catastrophic primary and secondary effects it generates, appears short-sighted and questionable.

ACKNOWLEDGMENTS

First of all, my sincerest thanks to all my sources in southern Ethiopia and Kenya; they patiently offered me a glimpse into their lifeworld. I am especially thankful to my dialogue partners and assistants from the ethnic groups of the Burji-Konso Cluster, many of whom became my friends and teachers. I have remained close to a number of them past my research trips.

They responded openly to my numerous questions, were interested collaborators, and allowed me to participate in their gatherings, which examined cultural concerns and legal questions, including the application of their laws. I will single out here Aceke Kalata, Battire Shudo, Dinote Kussia, Dorze Kayre, Picole Harso, Salle Chota, Ote Soke, and Shako Otto. I remain in close contact with Woche Guyo and Bogalle Takito as well as others. I was thus able to address questions to them from Germany and discuss their meticulous research.

I also owe numerous insights to the participants in the Thursday seminars on the philosophy of law at Ludwig-Maximilian-University in Munich. From among them, my particular thanks go to Heinrich Scholler and Ursula Scheubel for their clarification of juridical questions.

The present project was discussed and debated intensively in my postgraduate colloquium at the Institute for

Ethnology in Munich. My thanks to the participants for many important suggestions: Alexander Kellner, Florian Beck, Andreas Hirt, and Nicolas Grießmeier. Outside the colloquium, Werner Petermann gave guidance and support, Barbara Kleiner consistently offered a friendly ear for my questions and doubts, and Barbara Rusch generously provided a critical review and streamlining of the text. Thanks to Tilman Vogt for the scrupulous revision of the text.

NOTES

PART I

1. Supplementary material as well as further comments on the present text are available online as *Materialien zu Recht als Hort der Anarchie* on the open access server of the Ludwig Maximilian University in Munich at https://epub.ub.uni-muenchen.de/28399.

2. As ethnological research (cf. section I.5.3) shows, theirs is a legal system with its own historical development, and not at all an evolutionary forerunner of our own law, as some historians of the subject presume (including Wesel 2006, 15ff.).

3. Todorov 2001, 1.

4. "Jura autem Summae Potestatis sive Institutae sive Vi Acquisitae eadem sunt, … Itaque qui ea possidet neque puniri, neque Reus eri jure potest." Hobbes 1651 [2012 reprint], 307.

5. Jaspers 1947, 366, cited in Haude and Wagner 1999, 26.

6. Trotha 2011, 28.

7. Durkheim 1984, 327ff.

8. Evans-Pritchard 1940a, 1940b. For the description and analysis of this societal type, see section I.5

9. Barclay 1985, 254.

10. Boehm 1993; Sigrist 1986, 186.

11. Clastres 1987, 27ff.

12. Dahrendorf 1964, 84.

13. Sigrist 1978, 43.

14. Ratsch 1996, 58, citing Kropotkin 1898.

15. Cf. Marx, MEW 2:74, 3:282.

16. Face-to-face groups vary in terms of the number of members, depending, among other things, on climatic zones, territorial conditions, seasons, methods of hunting and gathering, and group traditions. It is important, however, that people know one another. The winter community of an Inuit igloo with five to six people may be considered the smallest type, while in warmer areas or in the warm seasons on feast days, several hundred people may come together. For the populous ethnic groups of the Horn of Africa, see section I.5.2.

17. For the history of this research, see, for example, Kramer and Sigrist 1978; Robinson and Tormey 2012; Amborn 2002a, 275. Beyond this selection, see Barclay 1985, chapter 3; Fortes and Evans-Pritchard 1940; Luig 2000, 13f., 29; Macdonald 2008; Sigrist 1978, 31; Sigrist 2004; https://sites.google.com/site/charlesjhmacdonaldssite.

18. Ethnological research revealed reciprocity to be a guiding principle and structural feature of "egalitarian" societies. It was Marcel Mauss's *The Gift* (1925) that inspired ethnologists to undertake further research.

19. Petermann 2004, 231. Rousseau's egalitarian noble savage then becomes a wild barbarian in need of civilization (in other words, subjugation and colonization).

20. Sahlins 1958, 1.

21. Concerning the role of women in southern Ethiopian polycephalic societies, Echi Christina Gabbert (2014, 201) writes,

> I have never shared the belief that [women] are victims, but have observed instead that the Arbore women in their role as mother and wife were respected above all—far more palpably than I have experienced in my own Western context. This respect generates the self-assurance necessary to be a critical, active, and

innovative member of society of a kind that only on first glance appears to be governed by men.

Much has been written about the significant economic and therefore also social status of the woman in many West African sedimentary societies. Here I will only mention the powerful women's federations among the Igbo. In 1929 they even rose up against the "warrant chiefs" installed by the British, as a result of which sixty women were shot to death (Akude et al. 2011, 199f.).

22. Cf. Max Weber (1978, 1134): "We might almost say that the normal condition of primitive communities was anarchy moderated by compliance with customs." Evans-Pritchard (1940a; 1940b, 296) examines this extensively under the term "ordered anarchy."

23. Cf. Amborn 2002a.

24. Akude 2011, 113, cited in Horton 1965, 164.

25. Graeber 2004, 89.

26. I was able to observe this myself during several stays in Ethiopia. Correspondence with native informants strengthened my impressions.

27. Sigrist 1978, 43.

28. Graeber 2004, 83.

29. Harvey 2001.

30. Cf. section III.3.3.

31. See, for example, articles from November 15, 1991 and September 15, 2014 in *VDI Nachrichten*, the weekly newspaper of the Association of German Engineers.

32. Sigrist (1986) is informative on the distribution and composition of acephalic societies in Africa. Volker Riehl (1993) offers an important case study from the postcolonial period in Africa of the Tallensi, who successfully adapted their acephalic model to changing societal and political circumstances.

Several authors have adduced further examples in a collection edited by Günter Best and Reinhard Kößler (2000). Andrew Robinson and Simon Tomey (2012) review recent works on self-organized social forms without hierarchical institutions. On anarchistic societies in the mountainous zones of Southeast Asia, see Scott 2009. James C. Scott (2014) shows in his book *Two Cheers for Anarchism* how people worldwide call hierarchies into question and practice creative alternative forms of conviviality. In southern Ethiopia and northern Kenya, I was able to witness the capacity of polycephalic societies to react to external political and social threats without abandoning their principles. Even in Bali, which is known for its hierarchical social order, I saw something relevant in 2003: in Tenganan, a polycephalic society had persisted from the time of the twelfth century. Even in the hierarchical environment of northern Ethiopia we find "islands" with egalitarian echoes.

33. Zimmering 2005, 1008.

34. Ibid. Stephen Nugent (2012) presents a further illustration; he considers the "landless people's movement" (*movimento sem terra*) in Brazil to be one of the most significant social anarchistic tendencies of the time.

35. Luig 2000, 29.

36. Ibid., 33.

37. Macdonald, 2008; https://sites.google.com/site/charlesjh macdonaldssite.

38. Sigrist 1978, chapter 8.2.

39. Graeber 2008, 54ff.

40. Bujo 2000; Eghosa Osaghae 2000; Kwasi Wiredu 2000; Amborn 2004; Amborn 2005a, 2.

41. The site mostlywater.org no longer exists, but its content can still be consulted on internet archives.

42. Robinson and Tormey 2012, 154f.

43. Robinson and Tormey (ibid., 154) conclude that "the struggle for anarchism is ... not a singular entity. ... Rather it is located in the practices, ethics, habits and modes of being evinced by a multitude of different groups and societies ... [in] a struggle for forms of life that refuse to obey the governing logic of the world system."

44. This was a more or less conscious emergence of a permanent discourse and expression of an ethos anchored in the habitus. A Burji at a Burji assembly stated this without reservations: "We have never had a king, and we don't want a king" (reported in conversation with Alexander Kellner).

45. Eckert 2004, 22f.

46. Over the last decade, this loose affiliation has left the informal sector and become a new, self-organized institution. See Amborn 2005a, 2006.

47. Thurnwald 1934, 5f.

48. Benda-Beckmann and Benda-Beckmann 2007, 15.

49. Benda-Beckmann, Benda-Beckmann, and Turner 2005.

50. The existence of multicultural societies in Germany, concomitant juxtaposition of value conceptions, and recognition of human rights discussion call for a legal compromise with "cultural difference." This does not so much pose the question of autonomous jurisdiction as of what minorities are entitled to *within* our legal system. Gabriele Britz (2000) examines the extent to which this matter deserves due consideration in our constitution.

51. Development of law from imperial ties until present, see Scholler 2008, passim

52. Ethiopian constitution of December 1994, Article 34, 5.5: "This Constitution shall not preclude the right of parties to voluntarily submit their dispute for adjudication in accordance with religious or customary laws." Article 78, 5. 5: "The Council of Peoples Representatives and State Parliaments may, in

accordance with Article 34 Sub-Article (5) of this Constitution, establish or recognize religious and customary courts of law."

53. Nicolas 2011.

54. Smidt 2007, 513.

55. See Schareika 2007.

PART II

1. Benjamin 1986, 277–300.

2. Ibid., 286.

3. Schmitt 1934, 946f.

4. Sorel, cited in Benjamin 1986, 291.

5. Comaroff and Comaroff 2007, 141, 146.

6. Cf. Diefenbacher 1996, 12.

7. Clastres 1987, 24.

8. Here some factors should briefly be mentioned: the economic and political influence of the industrialized nations on so-called developing countries along with the accompanying orientation toward Western educational models in schools and universities, contact with occidental cultures through migratory labor, urbanization, and emigration, and the expansion of scriptural religions and their attendant civilizing claims.

9. Dreyfus and Rabinow 1982, 208ff. See also Fink-Eitel 1994, part III; Petermann 2004, 1013f.

10. Foucault 1977, 219ff., 223.

11. Ibid., 223f.

12. Foucault 1978, 94f.

13. Ibid., 86f.

14. Foucault 1982, 273, 222.

15. Ibid., 220. Conceptualized in this way, power and power relations can only be grasped *in actu*. Cf. Foucault 1978, 93f.

16. Foucault 1982, 220.

17. Ibid.

18. Weber, cited in Arendt 1969, 37.

19. Arendt 1969, 88.

20. Both have earned her the critique that her arguments are divorced from reality. Even when she focuses on the political activity of free people within the polis, she is clearly conscious of the slaveholding nature of Greek society. Cf. Arendt 1958.

21. Arendt 1969, 44.

22. Ibid.

23. Cf. Gadamer 1975, 274f.

24. Arendt 1969, 46.

25. Arendt 1958, 32; Arendt 1969, 56.

26. Arendt 1958, 26.

27. Arendt 1982, 42f., 53.

28. Ibid., 10.

29. One of the most sensational cases that demanded reflective judgment was the trial against Adolf Eichmann in Jerusalem. At essential points, the judges could not draw on constitutional law, and were required to pass judgment on actions and circumstances that had never before been subject to legal proceedings, and thus for which no legal precedent could be invoked. See Arendt 1963a, 55f.

30. Zerilli 2004.

31. Arendt 1961.

32. Cf. Becker 1998, 170.

33. Arendt 1992, 74ff.; Zerilli 2004.

34. Zerilli 2004.

35. Personal communication from Alexander Kellner.

36. Arendt 1963b, 189.

37. Arendt 1969, 41.

38. Ibid.

39. For the last section, cf. Arendt 1963b, 256 ff., 273; Arendt 1961, 190; Arendt 1969, 42.

40. Arendt 1963b, 151.

41. Ibid., 151ff.

42. Becker 1998, 172f.

43. Arendt 1961, chapter 6ff.

44. Arendt 1963b, 224.

45. Becker 1998, 174.

46. Arendt 1969, 41.

47. Clastres 1987, 12, 22.

48. Ibid., 12.

49. Ibid., 32ff.

50. Ibid., 155.

51. Fink-Eitel 1994, 87.

52. "These three types of 'signs' share an identical fate: they no longer appear as exchange values, reciprocity ceases to regulate their circulation, and each of them falls, therefore, outside the province of communication. Hence a new relationship between the domain of power and the essence of the group now comes to light: power enjoys a privileged relationship toward those elements whose reciprocal movement founds the very structure of society. But this relationship, by denying these elements an exchange value at the group level, institutes the political sphere not only as external to the structure of the group, but further still, as negating that structure: power is contrary to the group, and the rejection

of reciprocity, as the ontological dimension of society, is the rejection of society itself" (Clastres 1987, 41–42).

53. Fink-Eitel 1994, 88.
54. Clastres 1987, 154.
55. Cf. Clastres 1987, 114.
56. For a comparative study that steps outside South America, see Clastres 1994, chapter 10. For Africa exclusively, see Straube 1964.
57. Clastres 1987, 188 (emphasis in original).
58. Cf. Fink-Eitel 1994, 85.
59. While Clastres does not consider himself a structuralist, his proximity to Claude Lévi-Strauss is undeniable.
60. Habermas 1993, 118.
61. Cf. Amborn 2005a, 5.
62. Habermas 1984, 101.
63. Ibid.
64. Cf. ibid., 99.
65. Ibid., 99, 70, 17 100.
66. Habermas 1990, 102.
67. Cf. Habermas 1990, 103.
68. This is Habermas's (1993, 32) Rule U.
69. Habermas 1993, 94.
70. Ibid., 121, 147f.
71. Habermas 1984, 330f.
72. Bauman 1993, 227.
73. Habermas 1984, 70.
74. Habermas 1993, 161f.
75. Ibid., 16.
76. Habermas 1996, 25f.

77. Ibid., 35.

78. Ibid., 147, 148.

79. Ibid., 369.

80. Cf. Habermas 1993, 119ff.

81. Ibid., 47.

82. Hornbacher 2006.

83. Habermeyer 1996, 136; Habermeyer 2006, 96.

84. Habermas 1984, 198, 48.

85. Ibid., 52.

86. Hornbacher 2005.

87. Habermas 1993, 45.

88. Ibid., 47.

89. Amborn 2001.

PART III

1. Asmarom Legesse 2006, xxiii, 101f.; Bassi 2005, 74, 245f., 277; "Qaalluu," EAE, vol. 4.

2. Abélès 1981; Abélès 1983, 12, chapters 3–4.

3. Abélès 1981, 48.

4. Cf. Amborn 1983, 310. In light of the many clans in Burji that can be described in part as lineages, I use the single descriptor "lineage elder."

5. In Marsabit, I observed a ganni mediating in a conflict between members of two political parties who had divided the diaspora for months. Cf. Amborn 2009, 218.

6. Amborn 1976.

7. See section III.2.

8. Cf. the 2007 film *The King Never Dies* by Élise Demeulenaere and Pierre Lamarque. See also "officiants" in the next chapter.

9. In Dullay, the designation is the *poqolho piyate*, or poqolho, of the territory.

10. Markakis 1974, 107f., 155; Donham 2002, 69; Amborn 1976, 159f.

11. An example are the sacred *hayle* fields associated with the poqolho in Gollango, where the cereals that have come down from early history were cultivated. The revolutionary regime interpreted this as slave labor for large landholders and divided the fields among the local *kebele* authorities. But no one used the land thus apportioned, which lay fallow until the end of Derg rule. For related developments in recent decades, see Donham 1999, chapter 2; James et al. 2002, chapter 3.

12. Daffa 1984, chapters IV.5 and V.

13. By "post," I mean here a set of responsibilities and privileges conferred by society (often for a determined period of time), including the expected or required comportments that it demands.

14. Asmarom Legesse stresses such long testing periods to assay the suitability of candidates to a post as an essential characteristic of Oromo democracy. Cf. Asmarom Legesse 2006, 257f.

15. The same is true for other powers, such as warding off epidemics.

16. Hallpike 1972, 49, 72; Watson 2009b, 121.

17. Amborn 2010, 37.

18. For the events that led to the rise of the Gibe states, see the next chapter.

19. Thus Hamdesa Tuso, Lamberto Vannutelli, and Carlo Citerni (1899, 172) describe the woma as *capo*.

20. "Yem," EAE, vol. 5; Straube 1963, 322, 328.

21. This woman's first son is the designated successor. Afterward, the regulus sacer may not marry any additional women.

22. Asmarom Legesse 2006, 102.

23. Ibid., 247f.

24. Abélès 1981, 57; Straube 1957, 186.

25. Abélès 1981, 52f., 57.

26. Sperber 1974, 64.

27. For the Burji-Konso Cluster, see Amborn 2010, 34.

28. Jensen 1936, 502.

29. Hamdesa Tuso, Vannutelli, Citerni 1899, 199; Amborn 2009, 222.

30. Jensen 1936, 387f.

31. The generation group system underwent a further weakening as a result of socioeconomic changes in the frontier situation in Burji. Cf. Amborn 1988, 756.

32. Amborn 2009, 245f.

33. I met D'once Guyyo for the first time in 1973. His bearing demanded respect, but he showed nothing of the arrogance that people in comparable posts often exhibit. Even after the revolution, he continued to be thought of as a person of authority.

34. Jan Assmann, cited in Kellner 2007, 171, 55.

35. Amborn 2005b. This happened occasionally, and was not without consequence, as the fate of the balabat Ha-pee from Burji shows.

36. Pausewang 1977, 18; cf. Amborn 2009, 188.

37. Bassi 2005, 282f. "Even a younger client who possesses no herds must be asked respectfully whether he would like to assist with the herds or guard duty. He cannot be ordered." Baxter 1965, 64.

38. A wealthy businessman friend from Marasabit enjoyed great regard for his generosity, but refused to play the role of the Big Man.

39. Moreover, misers are subject to material damages in socially acceptable ways, such as in Gollango through "raids." After a rich farmer violated rules concerning mutual aid in a particularly ungenerous way, a "horde" of younger men broke into his farm, tied the owner to a post, roasted corn and millet from his stocks, and drank his entire supply of beer.

    Trespassing and robbery? Not according to the local legal system, which finds nothing to object to in such a "raid." No one has a right to legal complaints concerning this mild form of collective spontaneous justice. To the contrary, when the victim himself told me this story, it was with good humor, and the general feeling was that he had deserved it, as he had violated the principle of reciprocity. It transpired, furthermore, that he himself had taken part in such raids in his younger years.

40. Watson 2009a, 186.

41. Andrea Nicolas's (2011) work also shows a remarkable stability of equality-oriented legal conceptions in the urban environment.

42. As Adam Kuper (1971, 23) remarks in this connection, "Most African councils ... move easily from political to judicial matters and back again."

43. Concerning birth control via the Gada system in times of need, see Amborn 1994, 175.

44. Klausberger 1981, 33.

45. Bassi 2005, 101f.

46. Haberland 1963, 477–481.

47. Klausberger 1981, 81.

48. For a detailed look at central Ethiopia, see Nicolas 2011.

49. It is not always clear from the ethnological reports on this subject whether informants are actually telling the truth.

50. In everyday life he enjoyed no special regard, but as an assembly participant he was not made to acknowledge his social status.

51. In the previous case, it was a complex, interwoven debtor-creditor relationship. A circular was drafted, and those involved were invited to share their comments.

52. Amborn 2005a, 7ff.

53. Originally the poqolho was not allowed to take part in the assemblies; in the imperial era, he was required to be occasionally present there in his capacity as a balabat in order to convey the instructions of the Ethiopian authorities. The poqolho was excluded from legal proceedings that only affected a single ethnic group and other purely internal matters even in the imperial era, and this continues to be true today.

54. Hallpike 1972, 66–71; Hallpike 2008, 112–124, 218.

55. Watson 2009b, 121.

56. Hallpike 2008, 125; Kimura 2004, 40f.

57. Hallpike 2008, 238f.

58. Watson 2009a, 185f.

59. Tadesse Wolde Gossa 1991; Abélès 1981, 51; Straube 1963, 179.

60. Already in his Galla book, Eike Haberland (1963) reserved a great deal of space for the Borana legal assemblies. For many details, see Asmarom Legesse 2006. Marco Bassi's *Decision in the Shade* (2005) is a monograph on this subject. No ethnologist who deals with the Borana overlooks this theme.

61. Beyond the sources referred to in this chapter, two recent titles should be mentioned: Hamdesa Tuso's (2000) work on the Arsi and Oromo in general, and Nicolas's (2006) look at the Tulama-Oromo committees. For *čaffee* gatherings, see "Čaffee," EAE, vol. 3.

62. Bassi 2005, 278, 282.

63. Ibid., chapter 12.

64. Cf. ibid., 277.

65. Ibid., 171, 241, 252.

66. Haberland 1963, 229.

67. Cf. Asmarom Legesse 2006, 97; Abdullahi A. Shongolo 1994.

68. Cf. the report from September 18, 2012, http://ardajila.com/?p=1380.

69. Cf. Bassi 2005, 100, 107. Both legal domains have had to confront the influence of nongovernmental organizations as well as Christian and Islamic missions that have attempted to impose their conceptions of law and value onto the Borana.

70. For the Burji, see Amborn 2009, section IV.2.

71. Klausberger 1981, 335.

72. It is significant that a loosening of the incest prohibition among siblings is currently under discussion in Western countries. Thus, recently, the German Ethics Board recommended to the legislature a partial repeal of punitive laws against incest.

73. Among the Baka, death is specified for both man and woman. Cf. Jensen 1959, 70.

74. Polygyny is generally widespread among the polycephalic societies of southern Ethiopia, with the first wife possessing privileges with respect to the others.

75. Interestingly, among the Dullay, theft of beehives is seen as adultery, with this conception being based on the symbolic equivalence of wives and queen bees or hives. The same punishment is thus enforced for both crimes.

76. Since according to the rules of the Gada system here, a man is frequently fit for marriage only on reaching the age of maturity, his generally younger wife may have one or several

lovers. This bond is often formally recognized. The woman's children belong to the household, and the husband is always the socially recognized father; biological kinship plays a subordinate role. Cf. Bassi 2005, 126f.

77. If a married woman commits adultery and exposes her lover to her husband, the lover will pay the husband an indemnity. When adultery is suspected, the presumed offenders must submit to an oath ceremony. If the wife suspects her husband of adultery, she will turn to her maternal uncle, who will, if they find confirmation, bring the matter before the committee of their lineage and that of her husband's. The committees will attempt to intervene, but can also press for divorce.

　　Divorce without adultery is not at all seldom and is unproblematic, so long as the wife has had no children. The maternal uncle will first of all seek out a solution, and if that fails, he will approve the divorce. If the couple has children in common, representatives from the man's and woman's lineages will intervene. Children from this marriage will remain in the father's household, while the divorced woman will return to her lineage. Disputes over material goods and other matters will be settled by the two lineages involved.

78. Kellner 2007, chapter D.I.

79. If a person steals crops during the ripening period, the owner may beat the offender without fear of reprisal.

80. Hallpike 2008, 132.

81. Ibid., 114.

82. John Hamer reports on the insubordinate behavior of an elder from the Sidama Gada system. He was meant to be a living example of the societal norms, and his offense against them led to public ridicule and loss of reputation. Cf. Hamer 1998, 145f., 151. In 1975 in Gollango, I was told of the dismissal of a hayyo by the assembly. Cases of this kind are unexceptional.

83. With the adoption of Roman statutes as the basis for the International Court in The Hague, these norms were substantially revised in the postwar period. This is particularly true for Article 7, "Crimes against Humanity."

84. Bassi 2005, 109.

85. According to an oral report from Alexander Kellner from 2010.

86. Amborn and Kellner 1999; Klausberger 1981, 83; Bassi 2005, 109f.; Hamer 1998, 140, 7.

87. Turner 2005, 487.

88. Bammann 2002; Turner 2005, 95.

89. Pankhurst 1990, 200f.; Gebre 1992, 59f.

90. Hans Wissmann, cited in Bammann 2002, 6.

91. Bammann 2002, 5.

92. With personal injury, the proceedings are similar, but do not take up so much time as with murder.

93. For a detailed examination of this practice among the western Oromo, see Bartels 1983, chapter 22.

94. For the Kafa, see Bieber 1923, 249, 257. For the dismemberment of "blasphemers" among the Gofa, see Klausberger 1981, 79.

95. Straube 1967, 207.

96. Graeber 2004, 100f.

97. Abélès 1981, 52.

98. For expropriation and the politics of expropriation in this connection, see De Schutter 2011; www.bbc.com/news/business-11991926.

99. Field usage rights in recent times have come under significant pressure from the government in Ethiopia and Kenya, to the detriment of the entire social order. Both countries demand that exploited land be registered to individual persons—in other words, taken from the community.

100. A father assigns a part of his herd to his sons, but remains owner of it until they marry. Cf. Bassi 2005, part II; Dahl 1979, 151.

101. This transethnic, transregional polycephalic union of craftspeople and salespeople in southern Ethiopia and northern Kenya, which extends beyond kinship ties and has the character of a guild, forms a bridge, because its members' methods of operating bring together the ethnic and legal perspectives of the populations in their environment while adapting negotiations to current modern demands. The example cited is paradigmatic of the discussion style of the participants, their manner of proceeding, and their approach to decision making in response to infractions that threaten the harmony of the society as a whole.

102. Bassi 2005, 184.

103. Among the fuld'o, I have seen how the election of dignitaries is often delayed when there are too few participants. Eventually those present will decide to threaten those absent with exclusion from the association because decision making is the responsibility of all.

104. On the Borana, see Bassi 2005, 188f. It is striking to European or US eyes how calmly these hours-long debates can proceed. The disciplined conduct of formal assemblies in Africa is frequently remarked on. See, for example, Gulliver 1963, 228f

105. On the Arsi, see Haberland 1963, 476f. On the Tulama, see Nicolas 2006, 17f. On the Borana, see Bassi 2005, 187f., 273.

106. Heinrich Scholler has indicated the importance of legal proverbs in Germanic law, and established the relation to Amharic or northern Ethiopian proverbs. According to him, instead of embodying concrete legal rules, they constitute a kind of principle comparable to adages based on experience. Cf. Scholler 1991, 141; Scholler 2002, 95, 104; Scholler 2006. "The African legal proverb encompasses and grounds ... a

process of assimilating the circumstances of life to the prevailing normative order." Scholler 2002, 98.

107. Scholler 2006.

108. Möhlig 2002, 32f.

109. Amborn 2005a, 10f.

110. Kellner 2007, 54.

111. Hallpike 2008, 220.

112. Bassi 2005, 189.

113. Kellner 2007, 99.

114. If a feud affects only those directly involved, this is the task of moderators (for the process, see especially Nicolas 2011). In cases with effects further afield in the society, larger committees are always responsible.

115. Bassi 2005, 193f.

116. For a description of the reconciliation ritual for crimes resulting in death, see Bartels 1983, 241–254.

117. For the evolution of law from the imperial period to the present, see Scholler 2008.

118. Klausberger 1981, 18.

119. Braukämper 2014, 11. *Ordinamento politico, amministrativo e militare per l'Africa Orientale Italiana*, in *Gazetta Ufficiale del Regno d'Italia* 91, April 1938, chapter V., § 94: "Dove sia previsto dagli usi tradizionali un Consiglio degli anziani, la sua costituzione è soggetta alla ratifica del missario di Governo."

120. Klausberger 1981, 15f.

121. Cf. figures 46 and 50 in Girma Fisseha and Raunig 1985.

122. Scholler 2008, 185.

123. On the outskirts of the large cities and in many towns, the poorer parts of the population have had dire experiences with the state courts and view them with suspicion. Frequently,

however, the expanding, multiethnic cities, unlike the rural areas, offer no other alternative. This makes them breeding grounds for magic practices and sorcery that seek to supplant the law, identifying and punishing wrongdoers.

124. Cf. Hamdesa Tuso 2000, 94; Nicolas 2006.

125. The Arusha in northern Tanzania showed the same reaction. Gulliver 1963, 232f. Arendt (1969, 42) offers similar thoughts: the acceptance of the verdict reached depends on public "opinion" and the number of those who share it—in other words, on the support and general agreement of the many.

126. Eckert 2004, 22f.

127. Bujo 2000, 56.

128. Hamer 1998, 142.

129. At issue here are first pertinent and correct arguments, and then the reality of the circumstances in play. As opposed to judicial investigations,the goal is not so much to ascertain whether the statement of a delinquent corresponds with the truth. At times, an oath is demanded here. The fuld'o dispense with this, too, but threaten sanctions for those who do not speak the truth.

130. Habermas 1984, 348, 329 (fig. 16); Habermas 1993, 155.

131. Kellner 2006. "Lying (*labbeed*) ... [destroys] harmony within and around people. ... [A] Burji proverb formulates this drastically: 'War only destroys a country, but lies destroy seven of them.'" Cf. ibid., 298.

132. Hamer 1998, 146, 151.

133. Neither do ethics in the least represent collective or "customary" morality, as Habermas affirms.

134. Hamer 1998, 137, 151.

135. Hornbacher 2005; Keller 2007, 17.

136. Gulliver 1963, 232.

137. For further examples, see Zartman 2000.

138. Kwasi Wiredu 2000.

139. Arendt 1958.

140. "An ethics is termed universalist when it alleges that this (or a similar) moral principle, far from reflecting the intuitions of a particular culture or epoch, is valid universally." Habermas 1990, 197.

141. An illustration of the ways people are encouraged to both make a name for themselves and act on the behalf of society comes from Kolme (West Konso). A well-off person remodeled a meeting place employed by the work group that he himself organized and supported, laying out three rows of seating made of large stone blocks arranged in a semicircle. In his will, the man specified that his *waka* (the monument for highly regarded deceased men) should be raised just beyond the final row.

142. Bourdieu 1977; Bourdieu 1998.

143. Habermas 1984, 388.

144. Habermas 1996, 148.

145. A society gives up this freedom, for example, when "the bonding force of communicative action wanes in private life spheres and the embers of communicative freedom die out." Ibid., 369.

146. Kwasi Wiredu 2000, 2, section 3.

147. Graneß 2000, 5, section 13.

148. Graeber 2004, 92.

149. Habermas 1990, 68.

150. Foucault 1980, 132.

151. Habermas 1993, 173ff.

152. Ibid., 120, 152ff.; Bujo 2000, 99.

153. In regard to Western societies, see Arendt 1969.

154. Bujo 2000, 73, 86; Zartman 2000, 222. Worth mentioning are the South African reconciliation commissions, which have

taken on themselves the revelation of crimes committed during apartheid. After face-to-face meetings with victims, the commissions offer amnesty to offenders who publicly confess their crimes and express contrition. Cf. Dewitz 2004. Similar efforts have been made by the Gacaca courts in Rwanda in their examination of the genocide from 1990 to 1994.

155. "It gives the sense that things are being done as they should be done." Moore 1978, 140.

156. Just 2007.

157. Girke and Pankhurst 2011.

158. Ibid., 245.

159. Thus Walter Benjamin's analysis of state societies, in which an independent legal corpus requires recourse to violence *beyond* this corpus in order to maintain itself and its effectiveness, is invalid for polycephalic societies. Cf. Benjamin 1986, 300.

PART IV

1. Neu 1992, 287.

2. Ibid., 291.

3. Ibid., 315.

4. Ibid., 317.

5. Lewis 1965, 39.

6. They were favored through the control of important trade routes to and from Kaffa. Cf. Mohammed Hassen 1990, 137, map 8.

7. "Gimma," EAE, vol. 2.

8. Lewis 1965, 39.

9. Cf. Mohammed Hassen 1990, 94f.

10. Ibid., 96; Lewis 1965, 109; 132.

11. After the leader of Jimma submitted to the Emperor Menilek at the end of the nineteenth century, Jimma preserved a significant degree of autonomy by paying a tribute to the Abyssinian ruler until 1932. Moreover, until the 1930s, the king of Jimma was involved in the slave trade, which made him quite wealthy. Those found guilty by the courts could also be sold as slaves.

12. Cf. Lewis 1965, 42.

13. For the communicative power of the many and the finding of law, cf. Arendt 1963b, 151ff.

14. See especially Allott, Epstein, and Gluckman 1969, 22.

15. Where this did occur, as in the polycephalic societies in the Americas, it generally ended in catastrophe.

REFERENCES

ABBREVIATIONS

EAE *Encyclopaedia Aethiopica*

MEW Marx-Engels-Werke, Berlin

SOURCES

Abdullahi A. Shongolo. 1994. "The Gumi Gaayo Assembly of the Boran: A Traditional Legislative Organ and Its Relationship to the Ethiopian State and a Modernizing World." *Zeitschrift für Ethnologie* 119:27–58.

Abélès, Marc. 1981. "In Search of the Monarch: Introduction of the State among the Gamo of Ethiopia." In *Modes of Production in Africa: The Precolonial Era*, ed. Donald Crummey and Charles Cameron Stewart, 35–67. Beverly Hills, CA: Sage.

Abélès, Marc. 1983. *Le lieu de politique*. Paris: Société d'ethnographie.

Akude, John Emeka, et al. 2011. *Politische Herrschaft jenseits des Staates*. Wiesbaden: VS Verlag für Sozialwissenschaften.

Allott, Antony N., Andrew I. Epstein, and Max Gluckman. 1969. Introduction to *Ideas and Procedures in African Customary Law*, ed. Max Gluckman, 1–81. Oxford: Oxford University Press.

Amborn, Hermann. 1976. "Wandlungen im sozio-ökonomischen Gefüge der Bevölkerungsgruppen im Gardulla-Dobase-Horst in Südäthiopien." *Paideuma* 2:151–161.

Amborn, Hermann. 1983. "Referenz und Abwehr. Der sprachliche Niederschlag der gesellschaftlichen Sonderstellung von Lineage-Ältesten in der Burji-Konso-Gruppe." In *Sprache, Geschichte und*

Kultur in Afrika, ed. Rainer Vossen and Ulrike Claudi, 305–329. Hamburg: Helmut Buske Verlag.

Amborn, Hermann. 1988. "History of Events and Internal Development: The Example of the Burji-Konso Cluster." In *Proceedings of the Eighth International Conference of Ethiopian Studies*, ed. Tadesse Beyenne, 751–761. Addis Ababa: Institute of Ethiopian Studies.

Amborn, Hermann. 1990. *Differenzierung und Integration: Vergleichende Untersuchungen zu Handwerkern und Spezialisten in südäthiopischen Agrargesellschaften*. Munich: Trickster Verlag.

Amborn, Hermann. 1994. "Wirtschaftliche und soziale Stabilisierungsstrategien südäthiopischer Feldbauern." In *Überlebensstrategien in Afrika*, ed. Michael Bollig and Frank Klees, 159–177. Cologne: Heinrich-Barth-Institut.

Amborn, Hermann. 2001. "Soul and Personality as a Communal Bond." *Anthropos* 96:41–57.

Amborn, Hermann. 2002a. "Ausgleichsprinzipien in polykephalen Gesellschaften en Afrikas." In *Das Menschenbild im weltweiten Wandel der Grundrechte*, ed. Bernd Schünemann, J.-F. Müller, and L. Phillips, 273–290. Berlin: Duncker and Humblot.

Amborn, Hermann. 2002b. "Concepts in Wood and Stone—Socio-Religious Monuments of the Konso of Southern Ethiopia." *Zeitschrift für Ethnologie* 127:77–101.

Amborn, Hermann. 2003. "Karé: Der Ernst ist ein blutiges Spiel." *Tribus* 52:48–66.

Amborn, Hermann. 2004. "Fährten der Erinnerung: Die Verknüpfung von Vergangenheit und Gegenwart in Südwestäthiopien." In *Studia Aethiopica*, ed. Verena Böll et al., 383–404. Wiesbaden: Otto Harrassowitz Verlag.

Amborn, Hermann. 2005a. "Ausgehandeltes Ethos—Eine Form afrikanischer Diskursethik." *Recht in Afrika* 8:1–21.

Amborn, Hermann. 2005b. "Polykephale Gesellschaften Südwest-Äthiopiens zu Zeiten der Sklavenjagden." In *Auf dem Weg zum modernen Äthiopien*, ed. Stefan Brüne and Heinrich Scholler, 1–28. Munster: LIT Verlag.

Amborn, Hermann. 2006. "Gaining Power through Ethos: Fuld'o, a South-Ethiopian Guild." *Proceedings of the International Conference of Ethiopian Studies* 15:15–23.

Amborn, Hermann. 2009. *Flexibel aus Tradition: Burji in Äthiopien und Kenia*. Wiesbaden: Otto Harrassowitz Verlag.

Amborn, Hermann. 2010. "Gada—Spurensuche bei den Dullay (Südwestäthiopien)." In *Schweifgebiete*, ed. Alke Dohrmann, Dirk Bustorf, and Nicole Poissonnier, 19–41. Munster: LIT Verlag.

Amborn, Hermann, and Alexander Kellner. 1999. "Burji Vocabulary of Cultural Items: An Insight into Burji Culture, Based on the Field Notes of Helmut Straube." *AAP* 58:5–67.

Angelbeck, Bill, and Collin Grier. 2012. "Anarchism and the Archaeology of Anarchic Societies: Resistance to Centralization in the Coast Salish Region of the Pacific Northwest Coast." *Current Anthropology* 53 (5): 547–587.

Arendt, Hannah. 1958. *The Human Condition*. Chicago: University of Chicago Press.

Arendt, Hannah. 1961. *Between Past and Future*. New York: Penguin.

Arendt, Hannah. 1963a. *Eichmann in Jerusalem*. New York: Penguin.

Arendt, Hannah. 1963b. *On Revolution*. New York: Penguin.

Arendt, Hannah. 1969. *On Violence*. New York: Harcourt.

Arendt, Hannah. 1982. *Lectures on Kant's Political Philosophy*. Chicago: University of Chicago Press.

Assmann, Jan. 1997. *Das kulturelle Gedächtnis. Schrift, Erinnerung und politische Identität in frühen Hochkulturen*. Munich: Verlag C. H. Beck.

Bammann, Kai. 2002. *Im Bannkreis des Heiligen. Freistätten und kirchliches Asyl als Geschichte des Strafrechts, und kirchliches Asyl als Geschichte des Strafrechts*. Munster: LIT Verlag.

Barclay, Harold. 1985. *Völker ohne Regierung. Eine Anthropologie der Anarchie*. Berlin: Libertad Verlag.

Bartels, Lambert. 1983. *Oromo Religion: Myths and Rites of the Western Oromo of Ethiopia*. Berlin: Academia Verlag.

Bassi, Marco. 2005. *Decisions in the Shade: Political and Juridicial Processes among the Oromo-Borana*. Trenton, NJ: Red Sea Press.

Bauman, Zygmunt. 1993. *Postmodern Ethics*. Hoboken, NJ: Wiley.

Baxter, Paul T. W. 1965. "Repetition in Certain Boran Ceremonies." In *African Systems of Thought*, ed. Meyer Fortes and Germaine Dieterlen, 64–78. London: Oxford University Press.

Baxter, Paul T. W., and Uri Almagor. 1978. *Age, Generation, and Time*. London: Hurst.

Becker, Helmut, ed. 1985. *Michel Foucault. Freiheit und Selbstsorge, Interview 1984 und Vorlesung 1982*. Frankfurt am Main: Materialis-Verlag.

Becker, Michael. 1998. "Die Eigensinnigkeit des Politischen. Hannah Arendt über Macht und Herrschaft." In *Macht und Herrschaft*, ed. Peter Imbusch, 167–182. Berlin: Springer.

Benda-Beckmann, Franz von, and Keebet von Benda-Beckmann. 2007. *Gesellschaftliche Wirkung von Recht: Rechtsethnologische Perspektiven*. Berlin: Reimer.

Benda-Beckmann, Franz von, Keebet von Benda-Beckmann, and Bertram Turner. 2005. "Revitalisierung von Tradition im Recht: Rückfall oder zeitgemäße Entwicklung?" *Juridikum* 4. http://www.juridikum.at/archiv/juridikum-42005.

Benda-Beckmann, Keebet, and Fernanda Pirie. 2007. *Order and Disorder: Anthropological Perspectives*. New York: Berghahn Books.

Benjamin, Walter. 1986. "Critique of Violence." In *Reflections*, ed. Peter Demetz, 277–300. New York: Schocken.

Best, Günter, and Reinhard Kößier, eds. 2000. *Subjekte und Systeme. Soziologische und anthropologische Annäherungen:*

Festschrift für Christian Sigrist. Frankfurt am Main: IKO-Verlag für Interkulturelle Kommunikation.

Bieber, Friedrich J. 1920. *Kaffa. Ein altkuschitisches Volkstum in Inner-Afrika*. Vol. 1. Munster: Aschendorff.

Bieber, Friedrich J. 1923. *Kaffa. Ein altkuschitisches Volkstum in Inner-Afrika*. Vol. 2. Munster: Aschendorff.

Boehm, Christopher. 1993. "Egalitarian Behavior and Reverse Dominance Hierarchy." *Cultural Anthropology* 34:227–254.

Bohannan, Paul. 1957. *Justice and Judgement among the Tiv*. London: Oxford University Press.

Bourdieu, Pierre. 1977. *Outline of a Theory of Practice: On the Theory of Action*. Cambridge: Cambridge University Press.

Bourdieu, Pierre. 1998. *Practical Reason*. Stanford, CA: Stanford University Press.

Braukämper, Ulrich. 2001. "Der 'Verdienstfest-Komplex.' Rückblick auf einen Forschungsschwerpunkt der deutschen Ethnologie." *Zeitschrift für Ethnologie* 126:209–236.

Braukämper, Ulrich. 2014. *Fandaanano: The Traditional Socio-Religious System of the Hadiyya in Southern Ethiopia*. Wiesbaden: ISD.

Britz, Gabriele. 2000. *Kulturelle Rechte und Verfassung*. Tübingen: Mohr Siebeck.

Brüne, Stefan, and Heinrich Scholler, eds. 2005. *Auf dem Weg zum modernen Äthiopien: Festschrift für Bairu Tafla*. Munster: LIT Verlag.

Bujo, Bénézet. 2000. *Wider den Universalanspruch westlicher Moral: Grundlagen afrikanischer Ethik*. Freiburg: Herder.

Bureau, Jacques. 1981. *Les Gamo d'Ethiopie. Étude du système politique*. Paris.

Clastres, Pierre. 1987. *Society against the State*. Cambridge, MA: Zone Books.

Clastres, Pierre. 1994. *Archeology of Violence*. Cambridge, MA: Semiotext(e).

Comaroff, Jean, and John Comaroff. 2007. "Law and Disorder in the Postcolony." *Social Anthropology* 15 (2): 133–151.

Crummey, Donald, and Charles C. Steward, eds. 1981. *Modes of Production in Africa: The Precolonial Era*. London: Sage.

Daffa, Paulos. 1984. *Oromo: Beiträge zur politischen Geschichte Äthiopiens. Der Wandel der politischen und gesellschaftlichen Strukturen von der segmentären Gesellschaft zur Militärherrschaft am Beispiel der Mačča Oromo in der Provinz Wollega*. Saarbrücken: Verlag Breitenbach.

Dahl, George. 1979. "Suffering Grass: Subsistence and Society of the Waso Borana." PhD diss., Stockholm University.

Dahrendorf, Ralf. 1964. "Amba und Amerikaner: Bemerkungen zur These der Universalität von Herrschaft." *European Journal of Sociology* 5 (1): 83–98.

Demeulenaere, Élise. 2005. "Herbes folles et arbres rois." PhD diss., Muséum national d'Histoire naturelle.

De Schutter, Olivier. 2011. "How Not to Think of Land-Grabbing: Three Critiques of Large-Scale Investments in Farmland." *Journal of Peasant Studies* 38 (2): 249–279.

Dewitz, Clivia von. 2004. "Die begrenzten Möglichkeiten einer strafrechtlichen Aufarbeitung von Systemunrecht." *Recht in Afrika* 7 (1).

Diefenbacher, Hans, ed. 1996. *Anarchismus. Zur Geschichte und Idee der herrschaftsfreien Gesellschaft*. Darmstadt: Primus Verlag.

Donham, Donald L. 1999. *Marxist Modern: Ethnographic History / Ethiopian Revolution: An Ethnographic History of the Ethiopian Revolution*. Oxford: James Currey.

Donham, Donald L. 2002. "The Making of an Imperial State." In *The Southern Marches of Imperial Ethiopia*, ed. Donald L. Donham and James Wendy, 3–48. Cambridge: Cambridge University Press.

Donham, Donald L., and James Wendy, eds. 2002. *The Southern Marches of Imperial Ethiopia*. Cambridge: Cambridge University Press.

Dreyfus, Hubert, and Paul Rabinow. 1982. *Michel Foucault: Beyond Structuralism and Hermeneutics*. Chicago: University of Chicago Press.

Durkheim, Émile. 1984. *The Division of Labor in Society*. New York: Macmillan.

Eckert, Julia, ed. 2004. *Anthropologie der Konflikte. Georg Elwerts konflikttheoretische Thesen in der Diskussion*. Bielefeld: transcript Verlag.

Eghosa Osaghae. 2000. "Applying Traditional Methods to Modern Conflict: Possibilities and Limits." In *Traditional Cures for Modern Conflicts*, ed. William I. Zartman, 201–217. Boulder, CO: Lynne Rienner Publishers.

Evans-Pritchard, Edward E. 1940a. *The Nuer: A Description of the Modes of Livelihood and Political Institutions of a Nilotic People*. Oxford: Oxford University Press.

Evans-Pritchard, Edward E. 1940b. "The Nuer of the Southern Sudan." In *African Political Systems*, ed. Meyer Fortes and Edward E. Evans-Pritchard, 272–296. New York: Routledge.

Fabian, Johannes. 2002. *Time and the Other: How Anthropology Makes Its Object*. New York: Columbia University Press.

Fink-Eitel, Hinrich. 1973. *Michel Foucault zur Einführung*. Hamburg: Junius.

Fink-Eitel, Hinrich. 1994. *Die Philosophie und die Wilden. Über die Bedeutung des Fremden für die europäische Geistesgeschichte*. Hamburg: Junius.

Flanagan, James G. 1989. "Hierarchy in Simple Egalitarian Societies." *Annual Review of Anthropology* 18:245–266.

Fortes, Meyer, and Germaine Dieterlen, ed. 1965. *African Systems of Thought*. London: Oxford University Press.

Fortes, Meyer, and Edward E. Evans-Pritchard, eds. 1940. *African Political Systems*. London: Oxford University Press.

Foucault, Michel. 1977. *Discipline and Punish: The Birth of the Prison*. New York: Vintage.

Foucault, Michel. 1978. *The History of Sexuality*. Vol. 1. New York: Pantheon.

Foucault, Michel. 1980. *Power/Knowledge: Selected Interviews and Other Writings, 1972–1977*, ed. Colin Gordon. New York: Pantheon.

Foucault, Michel. 1982. "The Subject and Power." In *Michel Foucault: Beyond Structuralism and Hermeneutics*, ed. Hubert Dreyfus and Paul Rabinow, 208–227. Chicago: University of Chicago Press.

Foucault, Michel. 1989. *The Order of Things: An Archaeology of the Human Sciences*. New York: Routledge.

Foucault, Michel. 1985. "Freiheit und Selbstsorge." In *Michel Foucault. Freiheit und Selbstsorge*, ed. H. Becker, 7–28. Frankfurt am Main: Materialis Verlag.

Foucault, Michel. 1991. *Die Ordnung des Diskurses*. Frankfurt am Main: Suhrkamp.

Gabbert, Echi Christina. 2014. "Powerful Mothers—Radical Daughters: Tales about and Cases of Women's Agency among the Arbore of Southern Ethiopia." *Paideuma* 60:187–204.

Gadamer, Hans-Georg. 1975. *Truth and Method*. New York: Rowman and Littlefield.

Girke, Felix. 2011. "Plato on the Omo: Reflections on Decision-Making among the Kara of Southern Ethiopia." *Journal of Eastern African Studies* 5:177–194.

Girke, Felix, and Alula Pankhurst. 2011. "Evoking Peace and Arguing Harmony: An Example of Transcultural Rhetoric in Southern Ethiopia." In *The Rhetorical Emergence of Culture*, ed. Christian Meyer and Felix Girke, 225–250. New York: Berghahn Books.

Girma Fisseha, and Walter Raunig. 1985. *Mensch und Geschichte in Äthiopiens Volksmalerei*. Innsbruck: Pinguin Verlag.

Gluckman, Max, ed. 1969. *Ideas and Procedures in African Customary Law*. Oxford: Oxford University Press.

Gluckman, Max, ed. 1973. *The Judicial Process among the Barotse of Northern Rhodesia*. Manchester: Manchester University Press.

Graeber, David. 2004. *Fragments of an Anarchist Anthropology*. Chicago: Prickly Paradigm Press.

Graeber, David. 2008 *Frei von Herrschaft. Fragmente einer anarchistischen Anthropologie*. Wuppertal: Peter Hammer Verlag.

Graeber, David. 2011. *Debt: The First 5000 Years*. New York: Melville House.

Graneß, Anke. 2000. "Der Konsensbegriff." *Polylog. Zeitschrift für interkulturelles Philosophieren* 2 (1998). https://them.polylog.org/2/fga-de.htm.

Gulliver, Philip H. 1963. *Social Control in African Society. A Study of the Arusha: Agricultural Masai of Northern Tanganyika*. London: Routledge and Kegan Paul.

Gulliver, Philip H. 1973. "Negotiations as a Mode of Dispute Settlement: Towards a General Model." *Law and Society Review* 7 (4): 667–692.

Haberland, Eike. 1963. *Galla Süd-Äthiopiens*. Stuttgart: Kohlhammer.

Haberland, Eike, et al., eds. 1964. *Festschrift für Ad E. Jensen*. Vol. 2. Munich: Renner.

Habermas, Jürgen. 1984. *Theory of Communicative Action*. 2 vols. Boston: Beacon Press.

Habermas, Jürgen. 1990. *Moral Consciousness and Communicative Action*. Cambridge, MA: MIT Press.

Habermas, Jürgen. 1993. *Justification and Application: Remarks on Discourse Ethics*. Cambridge: MIT Press.

Habermas, Jürgen. 1996. *Between Facts and Norms*. Cambridge: MIT Press.

Habermeyer, Wolfgang. 1996. *Schreiben über fremde Lebenswelten: das postmoderne Ethos einer kommunikativ handelnden Ethnologie*. Cologne: Neuer ISP Verlag.

Habermeyer, Wolfgang. 2006. "Ethik, Hermeneutik und Rationalität in der Ethnologie." In *Ethik, Ethos, Ethnos*, ed. Annette Hornbacher, 87–105. Bielefeld: transcript Verlag.

Hallpike, Christopher. 1972. *The Konso of Ethiopia: A Study of the Values of an East Cushitic People*. London: Clarendon Press.

Hallpike, Christopher. 2008. *The Konso of Ethiopia: A Study of the Values of an East Cushitic People*. Rev. ed. Central Milton Keynes: AuthorHouse UK Ltd.

Hamdesa Tuso. 2000. "Indigenous Processes of Conflict Resolution in Oromo Society." In *Traditional Cures of Modern Conflicts*, ed. I. William Zartman, 79–94. Boulder, CO: Lynne Rienner.

Hamer, John H. 1998. "The Sidama of Ethiopia and Rational Communication Action in Policy and Dispute Settlement." *Anthropos* 93:137–153.

Harvey, Neil. 2001. "Globalisation and Resistance in Post–Cold War Mexico: Difference, Citizenship, and Biodiversity in Chiapas." *Third World Quarterly* 22 (6): 1045–1061.

Hassen, Mohammed. 1990. *The Oromo of Ethiopia: A History, 1570–1860*. Cambridge: Cambridge University Press.

Haude, Rüdiger, and Thomas Wagner. 1999. *Herrschaftsfreie Institutionen. Studien zur Logik ihrer Symbolisierungen und zur Logik ihrer theoretischen Leugnung*. Baden-Baden: Nomos.

Hobbes, Thomas. 2012. *Leviathan*, ed. Noel Malcolm. Oxford: Oxford University Press.

Höhne, Markus. 2007. "From Pastoral to State Politics." In *State Recognition and Democratization in Sub-Saharan Africa*, ed. Lars Buur and Helene M. Kyed, 155–182. New York: Palgrave Macmillan.

Hornbacher, Annette. 2005. *Zuschreibung und Befremden. Postmoderne Repräsentationskrise und verkörpertes Wissen im balinesischen Tanz*. Berlin: Reimer.

Hornbacher, Annette. 2006. "Abschied vom Weltethos? Terror und 'War on Terror' im Licht kosmologischer und ethischer Selbstbestimmung auf Bali." In *Ethik, Ethos, Ethnos. Aspekte interkultureller Ethik*, ed. Annette Hornbacher, 391–425. Bielefeld: transcript Verlag.

Horton, James Africanus Beale. 2011. *West African Countries and Peoples, British and Native, and a Vindication of the African Race.* Cambridge: Cambridge University Press.

Imbusch, Peter, ed. 1998. *Macht und Herrschaft: Sozialwissenschaftliche Konzeptionen und Theorien.* Wiesbaden: Springer.

James, Wendy, Donald L. Donham, Eisei Kurimoto, and Alessandro Triulzi, eds. 2002. *Remapping Ethiopia: Socialism and After.* Oxford: James Currey.

Jensen, Adolf E. 1936. *Lande des Gada. Wanderungen zwischen Volkstrümmern Südabessiniens.* Stuttgart: Strecker and Schröder.

Jensen, Adolf E., ed. 1959. *Altvölker Süd-Äthiopiens.* Stuttgart: W. Kohlhammer.

Just, Peter. 2007. "Law, Ritual, and Order." In *Order and Disorder*, ed. Keebet Benda-Beckmann and Fernanda Pirie, 112–131. New York: Berghahn Books.

Kapferer, Bruce, and Bjørn Enge. Bertelsen. 2009. "Introduction: The Crisis and Power and Reformations of the State in Globalizing Realities." In *Crisis of the State: War and Social Upheaval*, ed. Bruce Kapferer and Bjørn Enge Bertelsen, 1–28. New York: Berghahn Books.

Kellner, Alexander. 2006. "Kontextualität und Sensibilität: Wahrheit und Lüge bei den Burji in Südwestäthiopien." In *Ethik, Ethos, Ethnos. Aspekte interkultureller Ethik*, ed. Annette Hornbacher, 275–312. Bielefeld: transcript Verlag.

Kellner, Alexander. 2007. *Mit den Mythen denken. Die Mythen der Burji als Ausdrucksform ihres Habitus.* Hamburg: LIT Verlag.

Kimura, Brigitta K. 2004. "An Archaeological Investigation into the History and Socio-Political Organization of Konso, Southern Ethiopia." PhD diss., University of Florida at Gainesville.

Klausberger, Friedrich. 1981. *Woga—Recht und Gesellschaft in Süd-Äthiopien*. Frankfurt am Main: Otto Harrassowitz Verlag.

Kneer, Georg. 1998. "Die Analytik der Macht bei Michel Foucault." In *Macht und Herrschaft*, ed. Peter Imbusch, 239–254. Berlin: Springer.

Kramer, Fritz, and Christian Sigrist. 1978. *Gesellschaften ohne Staat. Gleichheit und Gegenseitigkeit*. Vol. 1. Frankfurt am Main: Syndikat.

Kropotkin, Peter. 1898. *L'Anarchie, sa Philosophie, son Idéal*. Paris: P.-V. Stock.

Kuper, Adam. 1971. "Council Structure and Decision-Making." In *Councils in Action*, ed. Audrey Richards and Adam Kuper, 13–28. Cambridge: Cambridge University Press.

Kwasi Wiredu. 1998. "Democracy and Consensus in African Traditional Politics: A Plea for a Non-Party Polity." *Polylog: Zeitschrift für interkulturelles Philosophieren* 2. https://them.polylog.org/2/fwk-en.htm.

Kwasi Wiredu. 2000. "Demokratie und Konsensus in traditioneller afrikanischer Politik. Ein Plädoyer für parteilose Politik." *Polylog. Zeitschrift für interkulturelles Philosophieren* 2. https://them.polylog.org/2/fwk-de.htm.

Lewis, Herbert. 1965. *A Galla Monarchy*. Madison: University of Wisconsin Press.

Lewis, Herbert. 1989. "Values and Procedures in Conflict Resolution among Shoan Oromo." *Proceedings of the International Conference of Ethiopian Studies* 8:673–678.

Lewis, Ioan M. 1982. *A Pastoral Democracy: A Study of Pastoralism and Politics among the Northern Somali of the Horn of Africa*. Oxford: Oxford University Press.

Luig, Ute. 2000. "Der Kampf der Regenmacher: Geistbesessenheit, Macht und Magie in einer Tonga-Familie (Zambia)." In *Subjekte und Systeme*, ed. Günter Best and Reinhart Kößler, 13–34. Frankfurt: IKO-Verlag für Interkulturelle Kommunikation.

Macdonald, Charles J. H. 2008. "Order against Harmony." *Journal of the Finnish Anthropological Society* 33 (2): 5–21.

Malinowski, Bronislaw. 1926. *Crime and Custom in Savage Society*. London: Routledge and Kegan Paul.

Markakis, John. 1974. *Ethiopia: Anatomy of a Traditional Policy*. Oxford: James Currey.

Mauss, Marcel. 1954. *The Gift: The Form and Reason of Exchange in Archaic Societies*. London: Cohen and West.

McIntosh, Susan Keech, ed. 1999. *Beyond Chiefdoms: Pathways to Complexity in Africa*. Cambridge: Cambridge University Press.

Messing, Simon. 1985. *Highland-Plateau Amhara of Ethiopia*. New Haven, CT: Human Relations Area Files.

Meyer, Christian, and Felix Girke. 2011. *The Rhetorical Emergence of Culture*. New York: Berghahn Books.

Middleton, John, and David Tait. 1958: *Tribes without Rulers: Studies in African Segmentary Systems*. London: Routledge and Kegan Paul.

Möhlig, Wilhelm J. G. 2002. "Der Stellenwert von Sprichwörtern im rechtlichen Kontext bei dem Bantuvolk der Kerewe (Ostafrika)." In *Rechtsprichwort und Erzählgut. Europäische und afrikanische Beispiele*, ed. Heinrich Scholler and Silvia Tellenbach, 25–42. Berlin: Duncker and Humblot.

Moore, Sally Falk. 1978. *Law as Process: An Anthropological Approach*. London: Routledge and Kegan Paul.

Neu, Rainer. 1992. *Von der Anarchie zum Staat. Entwicklungsgeschichte Israels vom Nomadentum zur Monarchie im Lichte der Ethnosoziologie*. Neukirchen-Vluyn: Neukirchen Verlag.

Nicolas, Andrea. 2006. "Governance, Ritual, and Law: Tulama Oromo Gadaa Assemblies." *Proceedings of the International Conference of Ethiopian Studies* 15:168–176.

Nicolas, Andrea. 2011. *From Process to Procedure: Elders' Mediation and Formality in Central Ethiopia*. Wiesbaden: Harrassowitz Verlag.

Nugent, Stephen. 2012. "Anarchism out West: Some Reflections on Sources." *Critique of Anthropology* 32 (2): S. 206–216.

Pankhurst, Richard. 1990. *A Social History of Ethiopia: The Northern and Central Highlands from Early Medieval Times to the Rise of Emperor Téwodros II*. Addis Ababa: Red Sea Press.

Pausewang, Siegfried. 1977. "Die Landreform in Äthiopien." *Afrika Spektrum* 12 (1): 17–36.

Petermann, Werner. 2004. *Die Geschichte der Ethnologie*. Wuppertal: Hammer.

Ratsch, Ulrich. 1996. "Vom guten und bösen Menschen. Der 'wissenschaftliche Anarchismus.'" In *Anarchismus*, ed. Hans Diefenbacher, 52–66. Darmstadt: Primus.

Reiss, Michael, and Robert Höge. 1994. *Schlankes Controlling in segmentierten Unternehmen*. https://elib.uni-stuttgart.de/opus/volltexte/2012/7969/pdf/rei94.pdf.

Riehl, Volker. 1993. *Natur und Gemeinschaft. Sozialanthropologische Untersuchungen zur Gleichheit bei den Tallensi in Nordghana*. Frankfurt am Main: Peter Lang.

Robinson, Andrew, and Simon Tormey. 2012. "Beyond the State: Anthropology and Actually-Existing-Anarchism." *Critique of Anthropology* 32:143–157.

Sahlins, Marshall. 1958. *Social Stratification in Polynesia*. Seattle: University of Washington Press.

Schareika, Nikolaus. 2007. "Söhne des Feuers, Brüder der Milch. Politische Prozesse bei westafrikanischen Nomaden am Beispiel der Wodaabe in Südostniger." PhD diss., Johannes Gutenberg-Universität Mainz.

Schlee, Günther. 2014. "Department Integration and Conflict." *Max Plank Institute for Social Anthropology Report 2012–2013* 1:9–38.

Schlee, Günther, and Elizabeth E. Watson, eds. 2009. *Changing Identifications and Alliances in North-East Africa*. New York: Berghahn Books.

Schmitt, Carl. 1934. "Der Führer schützt das Recht. Zur Reichstagsrede Adolf Hitlers vom 13. Juli 1934." *Deutsche Juristen-Zeitung* 15:945–950.

Scholler, Heinrich. 1991. "Anknüpfungspunkte für eine Rezeption der abendländischen Menschenrechte in der afrikanischen Tradition." In *Menschenrechte und kulturelle Identität*, ed. Walter Kerber, 117–161. Munich: Kindt.

Scholler, Heinrich. 2002. "Recht und Sprichwort in Äthiopien." In *Rechtssprichwort und Erzählgut*, ed. Heinrich Scholler and Silvia Tellenbach, 89–108. Berlin: Duncker and Humblot.

Scholler, Heinrich. 2006. "Die Ethik des Sprichworts und die Richtigkeit des Normativen. Ein Beitrag zur Rolle des äthiopischen Sprichwortes im Lichte der Diskurstheorie." In *Ethik, Ethos, Ethnos. Aspekte interkultureller Ethik*, ed. Annette Hornbacher, 261–274. Bielefeld: transcript Verlag.

Scholler, Heinrich. 2008. *Recht und Politik in Äthiopien. Von der traditionellen Monarchie zum modernen Staat*. Munster: LIT Verlag.

Scholler, Heinrich, and Silvia Tellenbach, eds. 2002. *Rechtssprichwort und Erzählgut: Europäische und afrikanische Beispiele*. Berlin: Duncker and Humblot.

Schünemann, Bernd, J. F. Müller, and L. Phillips, eds. 2002. *Das Menschenbild im weltweiten Wandel der Grundrechte*. Berlin: Duncker and Humblot.

Scott, James C. 2009. *The Art of Not Being Governed: An Anarchist History of Upland Southeast Asia*. New Haven, CT: Yale University Press.

Scott, James C. 2014. *Two Cheers for Anarchism: Six Easy Pieces on Autonomy, Dignity, and Meaningful Work and Play*. Princeton, NJ: Princeton University Press.

Sigrist, Christian. 1978. "Gesellschaften ohne Staat und die Entdeckungen der social anthropology." In *Gesellschaften ohne Staat*, ed. Fritz Kramer and Christian Sigrist, 1:28–44. Frankfurt am Main: Syndikat.

Sigrist, Christian. 1986. *Regulierte Anarchie. Untersuchungen zum Fehlen und zur Entstehung politischer Herrschaft in segmentären Gesellschaften Afrikas*. Munster: LIT Verlag.

Sigrist, Christian. 2004. "Segmentary Societies: The Evolution and Actual Relevance of an Interdisciplinary Conception." *Difference and Integration* 4 (1).

Smidt, Wolbert. 2007. *Encyclopaedia Aethiopica* 3: 613.

Smidt, Wolbert. 2010. "Erd-, Baum- und Wassergeister in Tigray und Eritrea—religiöse Konzepte jenseits des Christentums." In *Schweifgebiete, Festschrift für Ulrich Braukämper*, ed. Alke Dohrmann et al., 94–116. Munster: LIT Verlag.

Solomon Gebre. 1992. "Conflict Resolution in Traditional Amhara Society." *Sociology, Ethnology Bulletin, Addis Ababa* 1 (2): 55–60.

Sperber, Dan. 1974. "La notion d'ainesse et les paradoxes chez les Dorzé d'Éthiopie méridionale." *Cahiers internationaux de Sociologie* 51:63–78.

Straube, Helmut. 1957. "Das Dualsystem und die Halaka-Verfassung der Dorse als alte Gesellschaftsordnung der Ometo-Völker Südäthiopiens." *Paideuma* 6:342–353.

Straube, Helmut. 1963. *Westkuschitische Völker Süd-Äthiopiens*. Stuttgart: W. Kohlhammer Verlag.

Straube, Helmut. 1964. "Beiträge zur Sinndeutung der wichtigsten künstlichen Körperverstümmelungen in Afrika." In *Festschrift für Ad. E. Jensen*, ed. Eike Haberland et al., 2:671–722. Munich: Klaus Renner.

Straube, Helmut. 1967. "Der agrarische Intensivierungskomplex in Nordostafrika." *Paideuma* 13: 198–222.

Strecker, Ivo. 2013. "Political Discourse in an Egalitarian Society: The Hamar of Ethiopia." *African Yearbook of Rhetoric* 4 (1): 98–105.

Tadesse Wolde Gossa. 1991. "Some Gamo and Konso Public Places and Their Social and Ritual Functions." *Proceedings of the International Conference of Ethiopian Studies* 12:325–339.

Tadesse Wolde Gossa. 2000. "Entering Cattle Gates: Trade, Bond Friendship, and Group Interdependence." *Northeast African Studies* 7 (3): 119–162.

Taylor, Charles. 1994. *Multiculturalism*. Princeton, NJ: Princeton University Press.

Thurnwald, Richard. 1934. *Die menschliche Gesellschaft in ihren ethnosoziologischen Grundlagen*. Vol. 5 of *Werden, Wandel und Gestaltung des Rechtes im Lichte der Völkerförschung*. Berlin: W. de Gruyter.

Todorov, Tzvetan. 2001. *Life in Common: An Essay in General Anthropology*. Lincoln: University of Nebraska Press.

Trotha, Trutz von. 2011. "Jenseits des Staates. Neue Formen politischer Herrschaft." In *Politische Herrschaft jenseits des Staates*, ed. John Akude et al., 25–50. Wiesbaden: Springer.

Turner, Bertram. 2005. *Asyl und Konflikt von der Antike bis heute: Rechtsethnologische Untersuchungen*. Berlin: Reimer.

Vannuetelli, Lamberto, and Carlo Citerni. 1899. *L'Omo. Viaggio d'esplorazione nell'Africa Orientale*. Milan.

Warnecke, Hans-Jürgen. 1992. *Die fraktale Fabrik—Revolution der Unternehmenskultur*. Berlin: Springer.

Watson, Elizabeth E. 2009a. "Debates over Culture in Konso since Decentralization. In *Changing Identifications and Alliances in North-East Africa—Volume I: Ethiopia and Kenya*, ed. Günther Schlee and Elizabeth E. Watson, 173–190. New York: Berghahn Books.

Watson, Elizabeth E. 2009b. *Living Terraces in Ethiopia—Konso Landscape: Culture and Development.* Woodbridge, NY: James Currey.

Weber, Max. 1978. Economy and Society. Berkeley: University of California Press.

Weber, Max. 2004. *The Vocation Lectures.* Indianapolis: Hackett.

Wesel, Uwe. 2006. *Geschichte des Rechts: Von den Frühformen bis zur Gegenwart.* Munich: C. H. Beck.

Wilson, Bryan R., ed. 1970. *Rationality.* Oxford: Basil Blackwell.

Winch, Peter. 1970. "Understanding a Primitive Society." In *Rationality*, ed. Bryan R. Wilson, 78–111. Oxford: Basil Blackwell.

Wolde-Selassie Abbute. 2009. "Identity, Encroachment, and Ethnic Relations." In *Changing Identifications and Alliances in North-East Africa*, ed. Günther Schlee and Elizabeth E. Watson, 155–172. New York: Berghahn Books.

Zartman, I. William, ed. 2000. *Traditional Cures for Modern Conflicts: African Conflict "Medicine."* London: Lynne Rienner.

Zerilli, Linda M. G. 2004. "Wir fühlen unsere Freiheit." http://republicart.net/disc/publcum/Zetrlli01_de.htm.

Zimmering, Raina. 2005. "Neue soziale Bewegungen in Argentinien." *UTOPIE kreativ* 181:1000–1016.